O Level

English

Helen Toner • John Reynolds

CAMBRIDGE
UNIVERSITY PRESS

CAMBRIDGE UNIVERSITY PRESS

Cambridge, New York, Melbourne, Madrid, Cape Town, Singapore, São Paulo, New Delhi

Cambridge University Press
c/o Cambridge University Press India Pvt. Ltd.
Cambridge House
4381/4, Ansari Road, Daryaganj
New Delhi 110002
India

www.cambridge.org

First published, 2008
Reprinted 2009

Printed at Replika Press Pvt. Ltd.

ISBN-13 978-0-521-72002-1 - paperback

CONTENTS

Preface

This book is written by two experienced examiners of GCE and 'O' Level English and is intended specifically to help students preparing for the CIE 1123 English Language Syllabus and also those who are teaching them.

The book is in two sections: Section 1 deals with the requirements of Paper 1 (Continuous and Directed Writing) and Section 2, which deals with Paper 2 (Comprehensive and Summary Writing). In both sections you will find information about key skills required for success, practice exercises, exemplar material for the different tasks and tips and advice from examiners. The book is designed to be used both as a textbook to help you to prepare for the examination and also as a study aid to help you to reach the best grade of which you are capable.

The list of people from whom the authors have received advice and assistance is far too long for them all to be included here. However, we would, in particular, like to record our thanks to Cambridge University Press India Pvt. Ltd.; to all the examiners and officers of CIE with whom we have worked over the years and from whom we have learnt so much and, in particular, to the thousands of examination candidates whose scripts we have marked and whose various skills and limitations have provided the basis for much of the advice in this book.

Acknowledgements

Extracts from *Neither Here Nor There* © Bill Bryson. Extracted from *The Lost Continent* by Bill Bryson, Published by Black Swan, a division of Transworld Publishers. All rights reserved.

Extracts from *Chocolat* by Joanne Harris, published by Black Swan. Reprinted by permission of The Random House Group Ltd.

Extracts from *The God of Small Things* by Arundhati Roy, reprinted by permission of HarperCollins Publishers Ltd © Arundhati Roy, 1997.

Extracts from *My Family and Other Animals* by Gerald Durrell, reproduced with permission of Curtis Brown Group Ltd, London on behalf of the Estate of Gerald Durrell © Gerald Durrell 1956.

Extracts from *A Goddess in the Stones* by Norman Lewis, published by Macmillan Publishers.

Extracts from *Himalaya* by Michael Palin, published by Weidenfeld & Nicolson Ltd., a division of The Orion Publishing Group (London).

Extracts from *The Millstone* by Margaret Drabble, published by Weidenfeld & Nicolson Ltd., a division of The Orion Publishing Group.

In Front of Your Nose by George Orwell (© George Orwell) by permission of Bill Hamilton as the Literary Executor of the Estate of the Late Sonia Brownell Orwell and Secker & Warburg Ltd.

The following is reproduced by permission of the University of Cambridge Local Examinations Syndicate.

	Subject/Paper Number	Month/Year	Question Number(s)
1.	1180/2 (Singapore-Cambridge GCE Normal Level)	September 1992	Section B
2.	1180/2 (Singapore-Cambridge GCE Normal Level)	September 1995	Passage only lines 1-10
3.	1115/2	June 2002	passage only
4.	1115/2	June 2005	passage only
5.	1120/2	November 1991	lines 1-14
6.	1120/2	November 1990	line 24, Q1(a)(i)
7.	1120/2	June 2005	lines 14-15, Q3(a)
8.	1120/2	June 2005	Adapted, new questions set
9.	1120/2	June 2005	lines 73-75,Q7(a)
10.	1120/2	November 2003	lines 21-45 edited, Q4(b), 5(b)
11.	1120/2	November 2005	lines 74-84, Q8
12.	1120/2	November 1990	lines 53-59 3dited
13.	1120/2	November 1991	lines 8-14
14.	1120/2	November 1990	lines 7-24 edited
15.	1120/2	November 1990	lines78-83 edited
16.	1119/2	June 1995	lines 74-86, Q5(b)
17.	1120/2	November 1993	lines 69-91
18.	1120/2	November 2005	lines 19 -25, Q3(b)

19.	1120/2	November 1996	lines 1-5,Q1(a)
20.	1119/2	December 1996	lines 54-69 edited, Q5(b)
21.	1119/2	December 1996	lines 36-46 and 51-57 edited, Q4(b) and 4(c)
22.	1119/2	June 1995	
23.	1120/2	November 1994	lines 10-20, Q2(c) and3(a)
24.	1120/2	November 1992	lines 7-11 edited, Q2(c) adapted
25.	1119/2	December 1996	lines 35-39 adapted, Q3(b)
26.	1120/2	November 1998	lines 31-36, Q5 and lines 62-64, Q7
27.	1120/2	November 1991	lines 3-6
28.	1120/2	November 1991	lines 26-34 edited
29.	1115/2	June 2002	passage only
30.	1115/2	June 2002	passage only
31.	1120/2	November 2005	line 1,Q9
32.	1120/2	November 2005	lines 35-56 edited,Q9
33.	Singapore-Cambridge GCE Normal Level	September 1992	lines 10-19, Summary question
34.	Singapore-Cambridge GCE Normal Level	September 1993	lines 15-23 adapted, Q7(a)
35.	Singapore-Cambridge GCE Normal Level	September 1993	text only
36.	1115/2	June 2004	lines 34-67, Q10
37.	1115/2	June 2005	lines 23-59, Q9
38.	1120/2	November 1999	Summary question
39.	Singapore-Cambridge GCE Normal Level	September 1995	Section D
40.	1115/2	June 2005	Q10
41.	1115/2	June 2005	Q10
42.	1115/2	June 2005	Q10
43.	1120/2	June 2004	Summary question
44.	1120/2	June 2006	entire paper and questions 1-11

Every effort has been made to trace the owners of copyright material included in this book. The publishers would be grateful for any omissions brought to their notice for acknowledgement in future editions of the book.

General Introduction

You are currently preparing to sit 'O' Level English Language and the purpose of this textbook is to help you to do the best that you possibly can. 'O' Level English is divided into two papers, Paper 1 and Paper 2, and, in order to reflect that division, the textbook is divided into two main sections, one on Paper 1 and the other on Paper 2. As you work with the textbook you will find explanations of the skills you are required to learn in order to do well in the examination, and you will be given exercises to help you to build up these skills in a progressive manner.

The syllabus contains twelve Assessment Objectives. The term 'Assessment Objective' refers to individual skills in which you must become proficient and on which you will be assessed, or judged, when you eventually sit the 'O' Level examination. It is useful to break down the syllabus into Assessment Objectives because it helps you to focus on particular aspects of the syllabus at any one time; it breaks down the syllabus into smaller sections with which you can become comfortable before moving on to other sections. Focussing on Assessment Objectives should make your learning progressive, less daunting and more meaningful. You will see a pathway to your examination result, rather than a frightening mass of learning where you are unsure even of a starting point.

Each of the two main sections of the textbook, that on Paper 1 and that on Paper 2, has a brief introduction in which the content of the Paper is described. Each introduction is followed by a number of chapters which are designed to take you through particular aspects of the syllabus, offering you explanations, exercises and links to the appropriate Assessment Objectives.

Each Assessment Objective is tested in either Paper 1 or Paper 2, and some are tested in both Papers. It is worth pointing out at this early stage that Assessment Objective (iii) requires you to show an awareness of how spoken and written communication varies according to situation, purpose and audience. There is no oral section in the examination which you will sit; however, it would clearly not be desirable to study English without speaking it, even if your study is not geared towards an oral examination. Consequently many of the exercises in this book are designed to be tackled with a partner or in a group. Your teacher will decide which of these exercises he or she wishes you to complete on your own, and which he or she wishes you to complete in pair or group discussion. Pair and group discussion are easy and enjoyable ways to learn to speak better English.

Chapter

Introduction to Continuous Writing in the Examination

Paper 1 is the Composition Paper. It lasts for 1 hour and 30 minutes and in total is worth 60 marks. There are two parts to the paper and you must answer both of them.

- **Part One** requires you to write a composition on one of a number of alternative subjects and is worth 40 marks. (Continuous Writing)

- **Part Two** consists of a task based on a situation described in detail, in words or diagrams and is worth 20 marks. (Directed Writing)

These two writing tasks will test your ability to 'communicate accurately, appropriately and effectively in writing'.

In order to demonstrate this, you will need to achieve the following Assessment Objectives:

i. recount personal experience, views and feelings

ii. use language to inform and explain

iii. show an awareness of how written communication varies according to situation, purpose and audience

iv. read a variety of texts accurately and with confidence

v. select, retrieve, evaluate and combine information from written texts

vi. appreciate the ways writers make use of language

vii. employ different forms of writing to suit a range of purposes

viii. plan, organise and paragraph, using appropriate punctuation

ix. choose a vocabulary which is suited to its purpose and audience, and use correct grammar and punctuation

x. write in Standard English

xi. spell accurately the words within the working vocabulary

xii. write legibly and present finished work clearly and attractively

Now let us look at how these Assessment Objectives are applied in the examination.

For Part One you will normally be given a choice of five different topics for the continuous writing task. You must write on only one of these. The topics will allow you to choose from descriptive, discursive, argumentative, personal or narrative writing tasks. Choose your topic carefully and choose the type of writing task that you are confident of doing well in the limited time available to you.

What are the key criteria and how are they assessed?

You are expected to communicate **accurately**. This will be assessed through how well you use correct Standard English spelling, grammar, punctuation and vocabulary in particular.

You are expected to communicate **appropriately**. This means that you should adapt your language and the content of your writing to meet the requirements of the task you have been set and to appeal to the specific audience for whom you are writing.

Finally, you are expected to communicate **effectively**. This means that what you write should be convincing and of interest both in content and style and that it is thoughtfully planned and organised in paragraphs to ensure that what you are writing is effectively and clearly communicated to your readers.

All the Assessment Objective listed above will be tested through the two different writing tasks contained in the examination. It is important that you prepare yourself sensibly for the exam; here are a few initial points you should think about.

Time Constraints

The time allowance for Paper 1 is 1 hour 30 minutes. During this time you must plan and write two separate tasks. You should not have any serious problems with completing both tasks in the time available but keeping the following points in mind may help you to do so effectively:

- It is suggested that you write between 350–600 words for Part One and between 200–300 words for Part Two. You should certainly not exceed the upper word limits as by doing so you will put yourself under unnecessary pressure. In practice, about 450 words for Part One and 250 words for Part Two should be adequate. Remember: you will be assessed on the **quality** of your written English, not on the quantity of what you write.

- Read through the question paper carefully before you start to write. Before entering the exam room you should already have some idea of the **type** of essay which you are most confident that you can write well under exam conditions. Look for those titles in Part One which specifically test this type of writing. Remember that you only have one chance in the examination – don't spoil it by deciding on a whim to attempt a type of essay with which you are not confident.

- Examiners frequently report that many candidates choose to write on a topic about which they have very few ideas and for which they lack the imagination and vocabulary range to write about convincingly. This applies particularly to those candidates who mistakenly choose the narrative or argumentative topics and run out of ideas after the first two paragraphs.

- Once you have decided on the title on which you will write in Part One, make sure that you have a clear understanding of exactly what is required of you; many candidates limit their performance by only partially following the instructions of the title and writing an essay not on the topic stated on the question paper but on something only loosely connected with it.

  Before starting to write Part One, be sure that you have a good understanding of the requirements for Part Two; it is a good idea to know what the task involves so that you plan how best to apportion your time.

- Spend some time planning before you begin to write. However, do not take planning to extremes – there is absolutely no need to write your complete essay out as a rough draft and then re-write it more neatly; doing this just increases the pressure you are under. However, you should make a plan of the basic structure of your essay and organise this plan into paragraph topics. It is a good idea to make sure that you know how your essay will conclude before you start to write it.

- Remember the reader: you are writing something which may be read by someone who lives in another part of the world and almost certainly belongs to a different generation and culture from yours. The more you can engage and entertain that reader, the more successful your writing is likely to be. Think about the sort of information you need to provide so that the reader can understand clearly what you are writing about; choose your words carefully to give as clear a picture of what you are describing as you can.

- You can best engage the reader by writing about something with which you are familiar; always try to set your essay within a context or background which is or could be within your own experience.

- Try to avoid relying too much on re-hashing other essays which you have done in preparation for the examination as it is very difficult to make such material fit the particular topic on which you are writing.

Standard English

The Assessment Objectives require you to write in Standard English and also to employ different forms of writing to suit a range of purposes. Let us look at these requirements in greater detail.

It is easy to misinterpret what is meant by the phrase 'Standard English'. It is not an instruction to write in an unnecessarily formal and over-literary style. However, it is important when you are producing a piece of continuous writing for the examination that you keep in mind the fact that the person for whom you are writing will be of an older generation and living in a country several thousand of miles away. This is not to say that your readers will not be familiar with teenagers and their attitudes (all examiners are or have been teachers), but they may not be fully up-to-date with the colloquial or dialect terms which you might use as a matter of course when speaking to your own friends. Standard English is the use of the accepted conventions of expression and grammatical usage which are common to speakers and writers of English of all ages throughout the world.

Writing to suit a range of purposes

- You should adapt your writing to meet the requirements of the particular task you have chosen and use a tone and register which are suitable to both your chosen genre and the audience for whom you are writing. This is something which applies to both sections of the exam paper. For example, the Directed Writing Task in Part Two will require you to use different genres from one year to the next. You might be asked to write a letter to a friend or to write a report of an incident for your Headteacher; the latter requires a different **format** from the former; it also requires a more formal **tone** in your writing as it is highly unlikely that you would write a formal report for your Headteacher in the same relaxed style that you would use when writing to a friend of your own age. Examiners will give credit to candidates who show that they have read the question sufficiently carefully to adopt a tone which is suitable for their purpose.

- **Warning:** Despite what has been said above, you should never forget that the ultimate audience for whom you have written is the examiner. She or he will give credit for adopting a suitable tone (for example, by choosing a fully appropriate valediction with which to end your letter or by introducing some convincing personal references in the body of the letter itself) but will be considerably less impressed if your letter consists of nothing but the abbreviations you might use when sending texts to your friends by cell phones as these are not Standard English usage!

- The essay topics in Part One are less likely to require you to write for a specific audience; however, it is important that you adapt your tone to suit the requirements of the particular type of essay that you are writing. For example, you need to consider whether writing the essay in the first person ('I think that…') is preferable to adopting a more formal or impersonal tone ('People think that…'). Again, if you choose to write the narrative topic, what style of narrative are you going to produce and what typical features of that style will most effectively suit the tale you are going to tell? If you choose the descriptive essay, should you write a factual or impressionistic description? Whichever you choose, it is important that you use a vocabulary which is suitable to your chosen approach and that your approach stays *consistent* throughout your essay.

- **Finally,** remember Assessment Objective xii – 'write legibly and present finished work clearly and attractively'. Although you are not marked for the quality of your handwriting it is important that the examiner can easily read what you have written. Illegible words and phrases result in the reader having only a partial understanding of what you are trying to say and this is likely to result in your being awarded a lower mark than would be the case if your answer was clearly written.

Chapter **2**

The Different Types of Essays

All questions in Part One are worth equal marks, which means that no one type of essay is considered to be easier or more difficult than any other. However, it is important that you are aware of the type of essay which you find most easy to write under timed conditions. The composition tasks set in the examination are of five main types; these are: Argumentative, Descriptive, Discursive, Personal, Narrative.

Argumentative Essays

An argumentative essay is one that requires you to put forward a point of view and to justify your reasons for holding it. You will be judged on how effectively you present your ideas through the ways in which they are structured and by the examples you use to support them. It is not usually necessary to try to consider in detail both sides of any argument but it is important that you develop your ideas logically in order to produce a convincing and persuasive conclusion. It is likely that you will write in a formal register although you should avoid sounding too pompous.

Descriptive Essays

Descriptive essays may ask you to write about a place or to describe a person or an event. The title will almost certainly give you the opportunity to describe somewhere or someone that you know well or an event which happened to you. (It is worth keeping in mind that the examiner reading your paper is unlikely to have a close knowledge of the person or place that you are describing and so the more details you can give in your writing, the more interest there will be for the person reading it.) It is likely that you will use an informal or even colloquial approach when writing this type of essay.

Some candidates mistakenly think that the best way to approach this type of task is by making up the person or place which they are describing; this is not a particularly good idea as it increases the difficulty of the task and increases the pressure which the writer is under. It is far better to spend your time thinking about choosing the most effective vocabulary and comparisons to bring alive the very special qualities of a place or person you know well, rather than spending this time in trying to imagine somewhere or someone who does not exist.

Discursive Essays

Discursive essays allow you to explore your ideas about a particular topic; they differ from argumentative titles because you are not required to develop your ideas logically towards a particular conclusion but instead to consider different aspects of a particular idea or situation. The examiners will be looking at how well you can consider the implications of the points you make and how skilfully you can relate them to the central topic about which you are writing. You may want to adopt a formal tone and an impartial approach to the topic but it is equally acceptable to write about it from your own personal standpoint.

Personal Essays

Personal essays are a mixture of descriptive and discursive essays and require you to write about something which you have experienced personally. It may be something like your first day at school or a family occasion in which you have taken part. Examiners will expect you to choose an actual occasion in your life and to give a true account of it. However, a successful personal essay depends very much on how skilfully the writer selects and organises details of the event being described: you may find that it is a good idea to re-order details in order to make them more interesting to your reader. Remember, that although the situation you are writing about may be very familiar to you, it will be necessary to provide some context for the events so that your reader is not confused. Personal writing can produce some very enjoyable accounts but the best are always carefully structured to achieve maximum effect.

Narrative Essays

Narrative essays require you to write a story and may either provide you with a sentence on which to base your writing or to ask you to write a story based on a particular situation. Many candidates choose this option as they think that it is an easy choice but, in fact, it is very difficult to construct and write a convincing short story within the time constraints of an examination. If you choose this topic it is important that you have a clear understanding of what the title requires before you begin to write and that you avoid writing too involved or too complicated a plot. Planning is very important with this type of essay as it is very easy to get caught up in the story which you are making up and then find that you have introduced so many twists and turns into the plot and so many interesting characters that you've actually got enough material for a three volume novel and nowhere near enough time to write it in!

Directed or Transactional Writing (Part Two)

The second part of the examination paper contains a directed writing exercise. Only one task is set so you do not have a choice of titles. This question is worth 20 marks in total; however, only 15 of these marks are given for your writing skills; the remaining 5 are awarded for including relevant content points as required by the wording of the question.

Directed Writing tasks, therefore, test both your writing and reading skills. It is important that you include all the content points required by the question in your response and that they are developed sufficiently to convince the examiner that you have understood what they involve. You will be expected to include them within a particular writing genre (a letter; a report; a magazine or newspaper article etc.) and you should try to write using a tone and vocabulary appropriate to the required genre. This task, in short, requires you to assimilate information and then convey it as clearly and convincingly as you can to a particular person or group of people using a specified style of writing. In preparation for the examination it is a good idea to become familiar with the key features of the style of the type of writing on which the question may be set.

Chapter **3**

Key Writing Skills

In order to write English confidently and accurately, it is important that you have a sound understanding of the technicalities of writing such as the different parts of speech, punctuation, spelling and grammar and usage. In order to ensure your understanding of these, the following sections contain the main details with which you should be familiar. There are also some exercises to test your understanding.

Parts of Speech

The different words in a sentence have different functions. In order to have a clear understanding of the mechanics of writing it is important to know the names of the different parts of speech and to be aware of their features.

> **Nouns**
>
> Nouns are *naming* words; they apply to the names given to persons, places or things.

The different types of nouns are as follows:

- Common nouns: A common noun is the name of any unspecified person place or thing, for example *girl, town, car*.

- Proper nouns: A proper noun is the name given to a particular person place or thing, for example *Leena, Mumbai, Toyota*.

- Abstract nouns: An abstract noun is the name given to something intangible like an idea, for example *thought, love, happiness*.

- Collective nouns: A collective noun is a single word, which describes a collection of things or people, for example *flock, team, audience, queue*. There is no hard and fast rule as to whether collective nouns should be considered grammatically as singular or plural. However, if the collection of things is functioning as a single unit then it should be expressed using the singular; if, however, the noun describes a collection of individuals functioning independently, then it could be expressed using the plural. Think of the difference between these two statements: *The team was playing well* and *The team were playing badly*.

> **Verbs:** are words which express an action or a state of being and are central to the structure of a sentence.
>
> For example: i.   The boy *kicked* the football.
>
> ii.   The tap *dripped.*
>
> iii.   The caterpillar *became* a butterfly.
>
> In each of these examples the verb is the word written in italics.

In the first example, the verb *kicked* is followed by the noun *football,* which is referred to technically as the object of the verb. A verb which is followed by an object is called a **transitive** verb.

In the second example, there is no object in the sentence and a verb like *dripped,* which is not followed by an object is, therefore, called an **intransitive** verb.

Finally, the verb in the third example *became* expresses a state of being and not an action. In this sentence, the subject of the verb *caterpillar* and the word following it *butterfly* refer to the same thing; the word following verbs like *become* is referred to as the **complement** of the sentence.

A **finite** or **main** verb is a form of a verb, which expresses an action or state of being, which is complete in itself. It has tense (past, present or future) and number (singular or plural); for example: I *walked* along the road. He *waits* for me at the corner. It *is* a fine day. There *are* no clouds in the sky. Tomorrow *will bring* both sunshine and rain. All of these simple sentences make complete sense and it is the form of the verb which ensures that this is so.

Another feature of a finite verb is that it can be in either the active or the passive mood. In the former, the subject of the verb performs the action ('The dog *bit* the man') whereas in the latter, the subject suffers the action of the verb ('The man *was bitten* by the dog').

Not all forms of the verb, however, convey a complete meaning and, therefore, need to relate to something else in the sentence. Such forms of the verb are known as non-finite. The most common **non-finite** parts of a verb are the **infinitive** (to laugh; to burn etc), the **present participle** (laughing; burning) and the **past participle** (laughed, burnt). When used in sentences, the infinitive functions as a noun – *He liked to laugh* and the participles usually function as adjectives – *The laughing man fell off his chair; The burnt wood was still smoking several hours after the fire started.*

Pronouns

A pronoun is a word used in place of a noun such as *I, you, he, she, it, we, they, this, that, anyone, anybody* etc. Use of pronouns prevents unnecessary and clumsy repetitions of nouns.

For example: 'Vijay and his sister went to the river to swim. When Vijay and his sister arrived there, Vijay and his sister found that the river was dried up.' By using pronoun the meaning would be more effectively expressed: 'Vijay and his sister went to the river to swim. When *they* arrived there, *they* found that *it* was dried up.

Adjectives

An adjective is a word used to describe a noun.

For example: The *red* house had a *huge* bedroom in which some very *naughty* children could be found.

Adverbs

An adverb is a word which qualifies (that is, adds to the meaning of) a verb, an adjective or another adverb. Many, but not all, adverbs end in –ly.

For example: i. The boy finished his dinner *quickly*.

   ii. I had a *rather* small breakfast.

   iii. The sun was shining *very* brightly.

In the first example an adverb is used to qualify a verb, in the second the adverb qualifies an adjective and in the third one adverb qualifies another.

Prepositions

A preposition is a word used with a following noun or pronoun to show the connection between persons or things. Common prepositions include: *about, above, across, against, along, around, at, before, behind, beneath, beside, between, by, down, during, except, for, from, near, off, on, over, round, since, till towards, under, until, up, upon.*

Articles

The word *the* is referred to as the Definite Article; the words *a* and *an* are known as Indefinite Articles.

Conjunctions and Interjections

A conjunction is a word used to connect words or groups of words.

For example: *and, or, but, however.*

An interjection is a word used to express a feeling such as joy or anger and is usually indicated by the use of an exclamation mark.

For example: (*What! Oh! Hurray!*)

Parts of Speech Exercise

Read the following passage and then complete the table below by identifying the function of each word in it:

It was raining heavily. Amrit was sitting indoors, eating a cake and watching television. He was bored as the television programme was dull and uninteresting. Oh, how he wished the rain would stop! However, the weather did not seem to upset his younger sister, Rita; she was sitting happily on the floor and reading a book that was full of brightly coloured pictures.

Nouns	Verbs	Adjectives	Adverbs	Pronouns	Prepositions	Conjunctions	Interjections

Sentence Types and Structures

Some definitions

A **phrase** is a group of words which does not contain a finite verb. For example: 'The dog, *lazing in the sun*, seemed thoroughly content with life.' The words in italics are a phrase beginning with a **present participle** and, in this case, they function together as an adjective describing the dog.

A **clause** is a group of words which does contain a finite verb. There are two types of clauses: **main clauses** and **subordinate clauses**. A main clause is a single unit of sense and can stand alone to make complete sense. For example: 'Salim ate his breakfast.' However, a subordinate clause does not make complete sense on its own; it is dependent on a main clause to which it relates; for example, 'Salim ate his breakfast *which he had cooked all by himself*. In this sentence, although the subordinate clause (in italics) provides further information about Salim's breakfast it does not make sense unless the reader knows the content of the preceding main clause. The word *which* is what is known as a **relative pronoun** (other common relative pronouns are *who* and *that*) and is used to join two clauses together.

A main clause, therefore, can, like the example above, function as a sentence. Such a sentence (consisting of just one main clause) is known as a **simple sentence**. A sentence which consists of two or more main clauses joined by a conjunction or conjunctions ('Salim ate his breakfast and then he left the house and walked to school.') is known as a **compound sentence**. Finally, a sentence which contains a mixture of main and subordinate clauses ('Salim ate his breakfast, which he had cooked all by himself, and then left the house to go to school which was on the other side of town.') is known as a **complex sentence**.

Just as it is important that you demonstrate that you are in command of a varied vocabulary it is equally important that you show that you can use a range of sentence structures to add variety and interest to your writing. Try to include a balance of simple and complex sentences so that you avoid monotony; in general, the more involved your ideas are, the more you are likely to use lengthy sentences. However, short sentences are often a very effective way to add emphasis to your writing.

Again, the type of sentence structures that you use will help to determine the tone of your writing. Consistently using complex sentences will create a formal tone which is suitable for argumentative essays whereas shorter sentences might well be more effective for a narrative essay. The ability to show control of complex sentences and structures in your writing, however, is one of the criteria the examiners are looking for in writing which is of top grade standard.

Sentence Joining Exercises

i.   Combine each of the following pairs or groups of short sentences into one longer sentence. You can omit words and alter the wording where necessary. Do not rely too much on the use of simple conjunctions such as *and*.

   a.   One afternoon I went for a stroll. The town was strangely quiet. There were very few people on the streets. The sky was of an ominous grey colour.

   b.   The school is situated in the countryside. It is an old redbrick building. It is easily seen amidst the surrounding fields.

   c.   Jasmine's mother works very hard. She cooks for all the family. She goes to the market every day. She wishes she could afford to employ a maid.

   d.   We were lost. We had been walking in circles for the last three hours. Every tree in the jungle looked the same. Night was starting to fall. It was growing dark.

   e.   Nissar was late leaving home. He drove his car quickly. He had a long way to travel. He had to meet his friends at the club. He knew they would not wait there for long.

ii.   Here is an episode of a story set out in note form. Tell the story in full using no more than three paragraphs and paying particular attention to sentence building. You may include additional details as appropriate.

   Mr Patel has a bad memory – forgets important details – arranges special celebration for wife's birthday – invites many friends and family members – hires town hall for the party – employs two top quality chefs to prepare food – books a popular band to play music – no expense spared – guests due to arrive at 7.30 pm –Mr Patel and wife arrive 7.00 – no-one else there by 8.00 – Mr Patel and wife are a little worried – by 9.00 – no-one there apart from Mr and Mrs Patel, the chefs and the band – Mr Patel in despair – decides to phone people – realises he has left cell phone behind – goes home to fetch it – opens up desk to pick up phone – discovers bundle of invitations – he had forgotten to post them.

Accuracy of Expression

Use Correct Grammar and Punctuation

To achieve a good grade in continuous writing tasks it is important that your writing is secure in the use of the main punctuation stops as this is one of the main requirements of the Assessment Objectives. Remember, the point of punctuation is to help the reader grasp the meaning of what you are writing; you cannot communicate clearly without using punctuation accurately.

The most important punctuation marks are:

Full Stop (.)

The full stop is used to indicate a long pause and to mark the end of a sentence.

Comma (,)

The comma is used to indicate a short pause; it should never be used to mark the end of a sentence.

Semicolon (;)

The semicolon is used to indicate a longer pause than a comma and is also used to link two main clauses with a common subject.

Question Mark (?)

The question mark is used instead of a full stop at the end of a direct question.

Exclamation Mark (!)

The exclamation mark is used instead of a full stop at the end of a sentence after making an exclamation. It is also used after an interjection.

Apostrophe (')

The apostrophe is used either to show possession or to indicate the omission of a letter or letters.

Speech Marks (" ")

The speech marks are used to indicate direct speech.

Colon (:)

The colon is used to introduce a statement or quotation or to act as a pause or balancing point between two balanced statements.

When punctuating a sentence never put in a stop at any place unless a pause is required in the reading.

A guide to the use of the more complicated punctuation marks follow.

FULL STOPS

A **full stop** is used to mark the end of a sentence. For example: 'It was a wet and cold morning in the middle of November. Padma, warm and comfortable beneath the covers, did not want to get out of bed.' Here there are two separate statements, each containing a main verb and each with a different subject; it is, therefore, correct to indicate the pause between them by using a full stop.

A full stop is also used to indicate words that are abbreviated when the abbreviated form of the word ends with a different letter from the full form of the word. For example: '3rd Sept'.

COMMAS

The following are the main occasions when **commas** should be used; the first six are purely mechanical, the other two require a little more thought.

i. To separate words or phrases in a list or series (except for the last two which are usually joined by 'and'). For example: 'In the kitchen there were a large oven, pots, pans, bottles, glasses and a stand containing cutlery.'

ii. To mark off the name or title of a person being spoken to. For example: 'Padma, there's someone at the door to see you.' or 'Excuse me, sir, you've just dropped your wallet.'

iii. To mark off words or phrases in apposition. For example: 'The restaurant owner, Mr Miah, is a very rich man.' or 'Mr Miah, the restaurant owner, is a very rich man.'

iv. To mark off words and phrases such as *however, therefore, by the way, nevertheless, moreover* etc. that have been interjected into a sentence. For example: 'At the same time, however, you should be very careful.'

v. To mark off phrases beginning with a participle when a pause is required in the reading. For example: 'My sister, seeing that I was upset, asked me what was the matter.'

vi. In conjunction with speech marks to indicate the beginning of a passage of direct speech: 'The teacher stood up and said, "……."

vii. To separate an adjectival clause beginning with 'who', 'whom' or 'which' from the rest of the sentence, when it is non-defining. This is a particularly tricky use of the comma, but the following example will help to explain the point: 'The Queen ordered that all the birds, which were sitting on the wall, should be fed.'

In the above sentence, the clause *which were sitting on the wall* must be non-defining and, therefore, implies that all the birds in existence happened to be sitting on the Queen's wall. However, if the commas were omitted, the sense would be that the Queen ordered that only the birds sitting on the wall were to be fed (those in the trees and on the grass were presumably to go hungry!)

viii. To break up a sentence into smaller parts and to help the reader to grasp the meaning. For example: Ajay, clumsy and awkward, stumbled into the room, knocked over a small table and then, before he could do any more damage, sank into the nearest chair.'

SEMICOLONS

A **semicolon** is used for two main purposes:

i. To separate two main clauses when a conjunction such as *and* or *but* is omitted. For example: 'Rita felt particularly tired that morning; she did not want to get out of bed.'

ii. To separate clauses or phrases in a list or series. For example: 'Salim jumped out of the chair; quickly walked out of the room; slammed the door behind him; searched for his bicycle in the garden and then rode off quickly to find his friends.'

COLONS

There are three main uses for the **colon**:

i. To separate two clauses where the second explains more fully the meaning of the first. For example: 'He was feeling very cheerful that morning: the sun was shining and it was the first day of the summer holidays.'

ii. To introduce a number of items in a list. For example: 'Before departure, please check that you have the following: passport, money, tickets, change of clothes and cell phones.'

iii. To introduce a speech or quotation. For example: 'Juliet: Romeo, Romeo, wherefore art thou Romeo?'

APOSTROPHES

The **apostrophe** is used for two main purposes; the first one is quite straightforward; the second is more complicated.

i. To indicate the omission of a letter or letters when a word or words have been contracted.

For example: 'I didn't do that. It's not true. You weren't there.'

ii. To indicate possession. In English the possessive form of a noun is shown as follows:

a. In the singular, the possessive form is made by adding –'s

girl   the girl's book

boy   the boy's hat

house   the house's windows

b. In the plural, when the plural is made by adding –s to the singular, the possessive is made by adding an apostrophe after the –s (s')

girls   the girls' books

boys   the boys' hats

houses   the houses' windows

> **Notes**
>
> i. When the plural of a noun is NOT made by adding -s, the possessive is made by adding -'s
>
> men   the men's office
>
> children   the children's toys
>
> women   the women's cars
>
> ii. The apostrophe is required in expressions like: a month's wait; a week's holiday; an hour's journey.

SPEECH MARKS AND INVERTED COMMAS

Speech marks (inverted commas) are used to enclose a passage of direct speech; that is the precise words which are said (or thought) by somebody. There are three patterns by which speech can be represented, as follows:

i. Anita's father said to her, "If it doesn't rain tomorrow, we'll visit the seaside."

ii. "Please, Daddy," replied Anita, "can we go even if it does rain? I'm sure it will stop by the afternoon."

iii. "I suppose we could," answered her father. "We ought to make the most of our holiday."

Notes

In the first sentence a comma is used before the words spoken. The first word of the direct speech has a capital letter.

In the second sentence the words "replied Anita," which break the direct speech, are separated from the rest of the sentence by commas. The opening word of the second part of this direct speech sentence does NOT have a capital letter, because it continues a sentence that has already started.

In the third sentence the two parts of the direct speech, separated by "answered her father" are complete sentences. For this reason "We" has a capital letter.

When you are writing a conversation between two or more people, remember that you should start a new line for each new speaker.

Inverted commas are also used to indicate the titles of books and films etc. "The Old Man and the Sea"; "The Pink Panther".

DASHES AND HYPHENS

The **dash** has a variety of uses. Its main use is to indicate an interruption to the planned flow of a sentence, for example by an afterthought or interjection. A dash is placed before and after the words interjected into the sentence – unless the interruption occurs at the end of a sentence when a full stop, question mark or exclamation mark replaces the second dash.

For example: "He showed me his new house – very nice it was too – that he had purchased from a famous celebrity."

"He showed me his new house that he had purchased from a famous celebrity – and very nice it was too!"

Another function of the dash is to indicate when a word or sentence is uncompleted.

For example: "The police made sure the identity of Mr S – was not revealed."

"Please, please don't – he begged, but it was too late!"

Finally, a dash can be used to indicate a sudden dramatic end to a sentence:

For example: "I'll tell you who the culprit was," said the detective. "It was – the Headteacher."

A **hyphen** is not a punctuation mark at all; it is simply a device for linking compound words together. For example, the phrase 'six-foot Guards' means that there are some guards who are six feet tall; on the other hand 'six Foot-Guards' means that altogether in number there are six Foot-Guards (soldiers belonging to the regiment of Foot-Guards).

The hyphen is also used to split a word into syllables when there is no room to fit the complete word into the space at the end of a line. In this case, the hyphen should always be placed between syllables, for example, 'walk-ing' but not 'walkin-g'.

The dash is distinguishable from the hyphen in appearance by being slightly longer.

Importance of Punctuation

Using punctuation correctly is important in ensuring that you communicate clearly. In order to achieve a C grade you should be able to demonstrate secure control of **full stops** and **commas** and **apostrophes**; in particular you should be able to use full stops confidently to separate sentences.

One of the features of a high level writing performance is the ability of the writer to use punctuation devices such as semicolons and colons to shape meaning and to produce particular responses from the reader.

Positive Punctuation

What are your thoughts about the way these three statements have been punctuated?

i. When she awoke, the rain was pounding down heavily on the roof of the house, Sunita decided that it would be a good idea to go back to sleep.

ii. When she awoke, the rain was pounding down heavily on the roof of the house. Sunita decided that it would be a good idea to go back to sleep.

iii. When she awoke, the rain was pounding down heavily on the roof of the house; Sunita decided that it would be a good idea to go back to sleep.

There is clearly an error of punctuation in the first sentence as the comma is not a strong enough punctuation stop to separate the two main clauses. The next two sentences, however, are correctly punctuated. In the second sentence the full stop is used to make two independent sentences and to **separate** the two main clauses. However, by a semicolon between the clauses in the third sentence, the writer has succeeded in giving equal emphasis to each part of what is now one unified sentence which skilfully combines the two main ideas.

Punctuation Exercise

i. Rewrite the following sentences using commas, full stops, semicolons, apostrophes and speech marks as required.

a. The journey can be made by road rail sea or air.

b. If for instance you want to buy a television set the best place to go is the electrical shop you can find this in the centre of town.

c. Sanjeevs books were lost somewhere in his fathers office

d. Excuse me sir can you tell me whats happened to my football?

e. Abraham Lincoln the President of the United States was assassinated while watching a play.

f. According to the Fahrenheit scale as you know water boils at 212 degrees on the other hand according to the Centigrade scale it boils at 100 degrees.

g. Many animals are renowned for their ferocity the tiger the lion the rhinoceros and the wolf are just a few of these.

h. He had waited all day for his turn it was now six o'clock in the evening and he decided it was time to go home.

i. We thank you very much for your hospitality said Rohit now we would like to wish you good night.

j. Have we far to go now? asked my sister from the back seat of the car I'm getting very bored with this journey.

ii. Provide the missing punctuation for the following piece of writing:

They had been driving for hours the countryside was flat and uninteresting and jamals attention as he sat behind the wheel of the old battered toyota was beginning to wander ahead of him he could see a shape like a hill although it was difficult to distinguish things clearly because of the mist which was rising from the ground in his mind he thought it could be a great castle maybe it was where the wicked witch was keeping the beautiful princess prisoner watch out suddenly cried out ahmed be careful what youre doing you idiot you nearly drove us into the ditch just now sorry mumbled jamal I must have been daydreaming

iii. Now write some interesting sentences of your own illustrating all the different punctuation devices explained above. You should try to show the different effects that can be achieved by being in control of punctuation.

Paragraphing

Paragraphing is one of the most important ways of structuring and organising your writing. When you are planning your essay, it is a good tip to plan your work by thinking about paragraphs and their topics.

Remember

You will be rewarded for writing essays which are clearly structured through connected and linked paragraphs.

All paragraphs should contain a topic sentence; i.e. a sentence which contains the main point of the paragraph. You can vary the structure of your writing by varying the position in which you place the topic sentence in different paragraphs. A good way to plan your work is through noting the different topic paragraphs you will use throughout the essay.

Once you have decided on your topic sentence, the rest of the paragraph should relate to it and develop from or towards it in a logical and coherent way.

Here is an example of a well-constructed paragraph; the topic sentence is written in bold type:

There is a strict dress code for the Golden Temple. First of all the head must be covered at all times. Scarves of various colours are readily available for non-Sikhs, either from any one of the 17 young lads who converge on you as soon as you pull up outside, or more cheaply from one of the stalls inside the forecourt. Shoes and socks must be removed. Hands must then be washed at marble-lined public basins and bare feet passed through a trough of water at the bottom of the steps.

Source: *Himalaya* by Michael Palin, Weidenfeld Nicolson Illustrated

In this paragraph, the first sentence is the topic sentence; it introduces the point about the dress code needed for a visit to the Golden Temple and the rest of the paragraph develops naturally from this point, each subsequent sentence adding further details which provide the reader with further information.

Exercise 1

Here is another paragraph from the same book only this time the sentences have been muddled up. Read through it and then re-write it in the correct order. You should start by identifying the topic sentence and then beginning with it.

One is entirely devoted to a chapatti production line.

When one side is done the chapattis are flipped over in quick, dexterous movements of a long thin implement with a half-moon end.

The piles are then removed and carried out to the refectory.

The kitchen is spread through several buildings.

A rat skips nimbly out of the way as fresh sacks of flour are cut open and fed into the bowels of a slowly turning machine, which regurgitates the flour as dough.

When the flipper is satisfied both sides are right he gives an extra strong flick, which sends the chapatti flying off the hotplate to land neatly on a pile on the floor.

One group of helpers rolls the dough into balls, another flattens each ball out into a pancake, and another lays them out on hotplates the size of double beds, made from cast-iron sheets laid on bricks with gas fires underneath, and capable of taking a couple of hundred chapattis at a time.

Source: *Himalaya* by Michael Palin, Weidenfeld Nicolson Illustrated

Exercise 2

Below are four topic sentences. Use each of them as the basis for a single paragraph of your own. Try to vary the position of the topic sentence by putting one at the start of a paragraph, one at the middle and one at the end. You could also write different paragraphs using the same topic sentence in different positions and consider the effects this achieves.

a. This is what I like best about my family home.

b. When it was all over, she quickly left the room.

c. This is the most memorable thing about the main street first thing in the morning.

d. When he woke up, it was the first thing he remembered.

Grammar and Syntax

Grammar is the science of language and involves the rules of standard written and spoken expression. Syntax refers specifically to the grammatical structure of sentences.

English, as everyone who speaks and writes it knows, is a grammatically complex language which is continually developing. This is not the place to give a detailed account of the grammatical structures of English but in order for your writing to convey its meaning clearly and unambiguously to an examiner it is important that you are thoroughly familiar with certain formalities of English syntax. Some of the main points of concern are described below.

Warning

In one of his essays, George Orwell listed what he considered to be some basic rules of good writing. Perhaps the most important one of these was the final one in which he advised his readers to 'break any of these rules, rather than say anything outright barbarous'! It is important that you keep this advice in mind at all times; rigid adherence to what are perceived to be the unfaltering laws of grammatical correctness can frequently produce writing which is stilted and unnecessarily pompous in tone. To take one simple example; some people believe that they should never use colloquial contractions (such as 'they're', 'you're', 'that's') in their writing. Certainly, such contractions may be out of place in a particularly formal piece of writing, but if you are writing a letter to a friend (for example as a directed writing task in Part Two, or an informal piece of description or narrative for Part One), not using such contractions would be likely to spoil the overall tone and register of your writing with the result that the reader would find it difficult to be fully engaged with what you are saying.

Errors of Agreement

It is important that subjects and their verbs should agree in number (i.e. whether they are singular or plural). Sometimes, especially in a complex sentence, it is very easy to forget this. For example, in the following sentence, the writer has forgotten that the subject of the sentence ('storeroom') is singular because of the number of plural nouns which come between it and the verb ('were'):

'The storeroom, full of books, broken desks and chairs, buckets, brooms and vacuum cleaners were very much in need of tidying up.'

Consistency in tenses

One of the most common errors made by 'O' Level candidates in their writing is to fail to write consistently in the same tense. A simple example of this is shown in the following sentence: 'I was feeling happy so I go to see my best friend.'

In this example, the writer has started in the past tense (was) and then changes to the present (go). This is incorrect and confuses the reader.

However, confusion with tenses is not always as straightforward as this example. Look at the following passage and decide what is wrong with it:

It is a very warm day so I decided to visit my friend, Vijay. The idea would be a good one as Vijay would live in a house near the sea and I think that we should visit the beach.

The tenses in these sentences are very confused indeed. The writer begins in the present tense, then slips into the past before using two unnecessary conditional forms ('would' and 'should') before coming back to the present again with 'think'.

Re-write the above two sentences first of all using the present tense consistently and then with the past tense. Which version do you prefer?

Other common errors

Wrongly used prepositions

Prepositions are words that are placed usually before nouns and before pronouns to indicate some relation, for example *in, on, to, at*. Using these precisely is an essential requirement of expressing yourself accurately.

For example, 'He fell by the telephone' has a different meaning from 'He fell on the telephone'.

Misunderstanding of singular nouns ending in —s

The items of clothing known as *jeans* and *pants* are grammatically plural forms and do not have singular forms; it is, therefore, incorrect to write 'He was wearing a pair of pant' and 'She spilt drink on her jean'.

Tautology

Tautology is saying exactly the same thing more than once, especially within the same sentence. For example, 'At the end of the outing the students returned back to school' and 'The true facts of the accident are these'. In these sentences the words *back* and *true* are unnecessary: *return* means to go back and *facts* are, by definition, *true*.

Spelling

As most students are fully aware, English spelling is difficult to learn because it is often irregular and, in particular, in many words, spelling does not give a simple representation of the spoken sounds. The following guidelines, however, may help you to avoid making some of the more common spelling errors.

> **Note**
>
> A prefix is a syllable added to the beginning of a word which modifies its meanings Similarly. a suffix is a syllable added to the end of a word.

- Words of one syllable ending in a single consonant following a single vowel double the consonant before a suffix starting with a vowel: *swim, swimmer, sad, sadden, bat, batting*.

- The last consonant is also doubled in words of more than one syllable if that consonant follows a single vowel and if the accent is on the final syllable: *permit, permitted, refer, referring, begin, beginner*.

- There is no doubling of the final consonant when, (i) the consonant follows double vowels or, (ii) when the accent is NOT on the final syllable: *conceal, concealed, proceed, proceeding, offer, offering, benefit, benefited*.

- When adverbs are formed by adding —*ly* to adjectives ending in —*l*, there is always a double —*l* : *full, fully, helpful, helpfully*.

- Words ending in a silent —*e* drop the —*e* before a suffix beginning with a vowel but retain it before one beginning with a consonant: *love, lovable, lovely; excite, exciting, excitement.* However, if there is a *c* or *g* before the silent *e* the *e* is retained before a suffix beginning with a vowel: *notice, noticeable, courage, courageous*.

- Words ending in –*y* following a consonant change the *y* into –*i* before a suffix: *baby, babies, fry, fried.* However, if the *y* follows a vowel the change to *y* does not take place: *monkey, monkeys, chimney, chimneys.*

- In words having the sound of 'ee', –*i* comes before –*e* except after c: *believe, receive, conceit.* (Exceptions to this rule are: *seize, counterfeit, weird.*)

- When prefixes such as un-, en- or in- are added to words beginning with 'n' a double 'n' occurs: *necessary, unnecessary, named, unnamed, numerable, innumerable.*

Tone and Register

Let us look more closely at two of the Assessment Objectives:

ii. show an awareness of how spoken or written communication varies according to situation, purpose and audience

vii. employ different forms of writing to suit a range of purposes

These refer to the tone or register of your writing or, in other words, to those features of your writing which give it its individual quality or style. For example, your tone could be described as formal or informal; humorous or serious and should be very much suited to the type of writing that you are producing. What is especially important is that your tone stays consistent throughout your essay.

The key features that go to making up a writer's tone are:

- writer's standpoint
- vocabulary
- sentence types and structures
- use of figures of speech.

Now we'll consider these features more closely.

Writer's standpoint

By this, we mean the attitude which, as a writer, you choose to adopt in order to present your ideas and character to the reader. The first decision to be made is whether you are going to use the 1st or 3rd person to express yourself. In general, if you choose to write in the first person ('I think…') you are likely to establish an informal tone as you are talking directly to the reader as an acquaintance. This informality of tone can be reinforced by the use of colloquial abbreviations ('I don't agree with this point of view' etc).

If you choose to write in the third person ('It is thought that…' or 'People think…') then your tone becomes more objective and impartial as you have removed the personal element and so you are likely to produce a more formal piece of writing.

It should be remembered that if you are writing a story, then the choice of narrative standpoint is particularly important as the decision to use a first person approach means that your story can deal only with events which can be known to and experienced by the narrator; if you choose to write using a third person narrative, you are in a position of having a more complex overview of the events in your story. Many writers of examination essays create significant problems for themselves when ending their stories by not thinking through the implications of their choice of narrative standpoint before they begin to write. Conclusions such as 'and then I died…' are seldom convincing!

Vocabulary

The proper words in the proper places Jonathan Swift

Never use a long word where a short one will do George Orwell

These two statements from two great writers of English remind us that having a wide enough vocabulary to be able to select exactly the word you need to convey a precise shade of meaning is an essential requirement for reaching the highest grades when writing an examination essay. However, it should be noted that neither writer suggests that good writing depends on showing off a wide vocabulary simply for the sake of doing so. English is a language rich in **synonyms** and the ability to be able to select the most suitable choice of words is a skill which all writers should aim to improve.

In your own writing you should always try to keep a clear picture in your mind of what you are writing about and then think carefully of the most effective words to convey what you are thinking about to your reader: in particular, well chosen verbs and adverbs are particularly helpful in doing this.

Vocabulary Exercise 1

Now let's look at an exercise to test your awareness of the shades of meaning in different words all used to describe something which you can smell. Use each of the following words in a different sentence in order to bring out its full meaning. You should use each word as a noun:

- smell

- aroma

- odour

- stench

- perfume

- stink

- scent

Vocabulary Exercise 2

Here is another exercise in choosing the best word to convey a precise meaning. This time you are required to look at adjectives and adverbs and should choose the most appropriate word from the different options you are given in order to produce a paragraph which describes a particular atmosphere:

- The street swarmed with (fierce/frantic) people all rushing (carelessly/ desperately) to reach their destinations. In the road, (angry/frustrated) motorists sat in their cars, (noisily/fiercely) sounding their horns in their hope to break up the (huge/unending) traffic jam. A policeman stood (bewilderedly/ importantly) on a (small/rickety) platform surrounded by traffic, his signals being completely ignored by all concerned. On one side of the road, sitting under a (tattered/colourful) umbrella to shelter him from the (burning/ relentless) sun, sat an (old/aged) man who was watching the scene with (detached/amused) interest.

> **Note**
> None of these words is wrong; you are being asked to choose those you think describe the scene with most clarity. You should also aim to produce a description which is consistent in its tone.

Confusions

Many writers of English blur the communication of what they want to say by confusing words which either sound similar to another one or which have a similar but not exactly equivalent meaning. Some of these words are listed below. Write sentences with each of them to make their meaning clear.

> **Note**
> You may need to use a dictionary to check the meaning of some or all of them.

avoid/prevent

stay/live

bring/take

uninterested/disinterested

bored/boring

there/their/they're

your/you're

horde/hoard

principal/principle

affect/effect

Figures of Speech

Another way to make your writing interesting is by making use of figures of speech such as similes and metaphors as these can add depth and detail to what you intend to say.

A **simile** is a comparison introduced by the words *like* or *as*, in which things, actions, people etc. are compared with other things etc. of a totally different kind. For example: 'The teacher surged into the classroom *like a stately galleon in full sail.*'

A **metaphor** is a kind of concentrated simile in which a comparison is made by saying that one thing is actually another thing of a totally different kind; for example: 'The banner of smoke flew proudly from the factory chimney.' Instead of saying that the smoke from the chimney looked like a large flag flying from it (which would be using a simile) the use of the metaphor makes the smoke and the banner one and the same thing, with the result that the comparison is more immediate in its effect.

It is important, however, that you use such figures of speech selectively and thoughtfully. Try to be original in your use of similes and avoid using clichéd comparisons such as *he ran like the wind*. However, you should also make sure that there are clear points of comparison between the two elements of your similes. It is also a good idea not to overdo the use of similes as too many will have the effect of clogging up your writing – remember, be selective and always think about what might be the effect on the reader of the stylistic choices you have made.

Your choice of similes and comparisons should give an indication of your personality as a writer and is, therefore, another way of establishing the individual tone of your writing.

Chapter **4**

Descriptive Writing

The first of the Assessment Objectives (see page 1) requires you to recount personal experience, views and feelings. This is tested in Part One of Paper 1 of the examination.

You will be presented with a selection of five titles from which you must choose one to write about. These titles will cover a range of different types of writing. However, the central requirement is that you write about your personal experiences or opinions; you do not have to pretend to be someone you are not in order to impress an examiner.

When you are thinking about which topic you should choose to write about, try to keep the following points in mind:

- you only have a limited time (about one hour) to plan and write your essay

- planning is important but do not produce an over-elaborate plan

- choose a topic which does not require you to spend too long thinking about what you should write – as far as possible write about something with which you are closely familiar

- you should be aware of the type of writing at which you do best; try to choose the topic which lets you write this type of essay

- remember that you will be marked as much on how you express yourself as on the content of your essay.

In general, this section of the exam paper will test the following types of writing: descriptive writing; argumentative writing; discursive writing; personal account; narrative writing. All of these will allow you to present your own personal views and feelings. Sometimes, one title will cover more than one type of writing. Here is a selection of essay titles from a recent examination paper with the type of writing each requires indicated in brackets:

  i. Describe a great celebration that you took part in. (Personal descriptive)

 ii. Write about an occasion when a special family meal produced unexpected results. (Descriptive/narrative)

iii. One day you made a bad mistake which upset other people. Write about how you tried to put things right. (Personal narrative)

iv. Should we worry so much about endangered species? What is your view? (Argumentative/discursive)

v. Write about the rivalry between two elderly people. (Narrative)

As you can see, no matter what type of writing is required at least four of these topics allow you to write from your direct personal experience. Topic v provides the opportunity to make up a fictional narrative if you wish, but there's no reason why you could not write about the rivalry between two people you actually know, if that seems appropriate.

Now let us look at these different types of writing more closely.

Descriptive Writing

The descriptive topic is in some ways one of the more straightforward pieces of writing to choose to do under examination conditions and allows you to write about something with which you are familiar and which is likely to capture the interest of the examiner who is reading it. There are different types of descriptive essay topics:

- A description of a place or a scene or a building

- A description of an event or an occasion

- A description of a person or an animal.

This is a fairly simple list and you can almost certainly think of other variations. However, the common factor is that in all of them, you can write personally about your perception of what is being described. When you are writing under examination conditions and pressure, it is much better to write about something or someone that is familiar to you, than to worry about having to make something up.

Exercise 1

Here are some examples of different types of descriptive writing. Read through each of them carefully and, in discussion with a partner, decide on the features that make them effective passages of descriptive writing. List examples of words and phrases and explain why they help to convey the scene or people being described to the readers. Try to describe and comment on the writers' tone of voice. Do not read the comments which follow until you have done this.

Passage: (a) Kundili

We arrived at Kundili after a four-hour drive to find a seething multitude, drawn from a number of tribes, gathered into a mile-wide dust bowl at the conjunction of the main road into Andhra Pradesh and a number of country byways leading down from the hills. Under the hard forthright midday sun it was a sight to guarantee eye-strain and eventual headaches. The sky was bleached white, with drifts in it of what appeared at first as red smoke blowing across, but which proved to be the blood-red dust, which lay a quarter-inch deep on every surface, caught up by the gusting wind. When the dust was blown across the sun it turned dark, swelled up and seemed to tremble. From all points of the market came the piercing glitter of metal articles for sale, from sheets of corrugated iron, pots and pans, and above all from the rows of polished aluminium receptacles for sale.

Source: *A Goddess in the Stones* by Norman Lewis, Picador

Passage: (b) Istanbul

Sighing, I smeared a little of the brown water around my face, then went out to see Istanbul. It is the noisiest, dirtiest, busiest city I've ever seen. Everywhere there is noise – car horns tooting, sirens shrilling, people shouting, muezzins wailing, ferries on the Bosphorus sounding their booming horns. Everywhere, too, there is ceaseless activity – people pushing carts, carrying trays of food or coffee, humping huge and ungainly loads (I saw one guy with a sofa on his back), people every five feet selling something: lottery tickets, wrist-watches, cigarettes, replica perfumes.

Every few paces people come up to you wanting to shine your shoes, sell you postcards or guidebooks, lead you to their brother's carpet shop or otherwise induce you to part with some trifling sum of money. Along the Galata Bridge, swarming with

pedestrians, beggars and load bearers, amateur fishermen stood pulling the most poisoned-looking fish I ever hope to see from the oily waters below. At the end of the bridge two guys were crossing the street to Sirkeci Station, threading their way through the traffic leading brown bears on leashes. No one gave them a second glance. Istanbul is, in short, one of those great and exhilarating cities where almost anything seems possible.

The one truly unbearable thing in the city is the Turkish pop music. It is inescapable. It assaults you from every restaurant doorway, from every lemonade stand, from every passing cab. If you can imagine a man having an operation without anaesthetic to a background accompaniment of frantic sitar-playing, you will have some idea of what popular Turkish music is like.

I wandered around for a couple of hours, impressed by the tumult, amazed that in one place there could be so much activity. I walked past the Blue Mosque and Aya Sofia, peeling postcard salesmen from my sleeve as I went, and tried to go to Topkapi, but it was closed. I headed instead for what I thought was the national archaeological museum, but I somehow missed it and found myself presently at the entrance to a large, inviting and miraculously tranquil park, the Giilhane. It was full of cool shade and happy families. There was a free zoo, evidently much loved by children, and somewhere a cafe playing Turkish torture music, but softly enough to be tolerable.

At the bottom of a gently sloping central avenue, the park ended in a sudden and stunning view of the Bosphorus, glittery and blue. I took a seat at an open-air taverna, ordered a coke and gazed across the water to the white houses gleaming on the brown hillside of Uskiidar two miles across the strait. Distant cars glinted in the hot sunshine and ferries plied doggedly back and forth across the Bosphorus and on out to the distant Princes' Islands, adrift in a bluish haze. It was beautiful and a perfect place to stop.

Source: *Neither Here Nor There* by Bill Bryson, Black Swan

Passage: (c) Train to Lahore

Porters cluster around us and a thin-faced ascetic old man with a Gandalf-like white beard grabs one of my cases, hoists the other onto his head and, a little disappointed that I choose to carry my own shoulder bag, marches off through the crowds.

Our driver nods approvingly. This old man is a great character, he says. He was carrying bags for British officers before independence. That was 55 years ago.

There are three classes on the train, two with air-con and one without. We're in air-con, 2nd class and are made comfortable by an army of solicitous attendants marshalled by a man in a white suit, green peaked hat and a crimson arm band, grandly embroidered with the words Conductor Guard. A rich cast of characters, all with titles clearly inscribed on jackets or lapels, come through offering refreshment of various kinds. My favourite is the Iceman, a stocky, embattled figure in a frayed white jacket, whose bulbous eyes and droopy moustache remind me of a small-time crook in a French gangster movie. He hauls a huge bucket in which is a block of ice with bottles squeezed around it. There is a tired, emaciated Sweet Seller and various perkier, smartly turned-out young men described on their lapel badges as either Buttlers (sic) or Waiters. Waiter No. 14 brings chai, sweet milky tea, and Buttler No. 7 collects the money.

Source: *Himalaya* by Michael Palin, Weidenfeld Nicolson Illustrated

All of these extracts describe either places or people and all of them are written in the first person and therefore record a personal response. Despite the differences of the characters of the writers which appear in the extracts, there are several similarities between the passages. All of them concentrate on focusing on precise details of the scene or characters they are describing. In extract (a) the details are particularly concerned with the descriptions of the 'piercing glitter' of the articles which are on sale; extract (b) contains both detail and the writer's reactions to and feelings about the city he is describing and in extract (c) the character of the Iceman is conveyed in particular through the details of his physical description with which we are provided.

Tools for Descriptive Writing

In order to bring a scene alive for the reader, it is a good idea to think about ways of describing how it appeals to the different senses such as smell and hearing. Effective descriptive writing makes use of certain linguistic devices which help to make clear what is being described. Among these devices are: similes, metaphors, adjectives. Another way to ensure that your descriptions are as precise and effective as possible is to think carefully about your choice of verbs and the adverbs which describe them.

Examples of these devices and their effects in the printed extracts are:

- **Simile:** For example, a Gandalf-like white beard (Gandalf is a wizard in *The Lord of the Rings*)
- **Metaphor:** For example, the sky was bleached white
- **Adjectives:** For example, the blood-red dust
- **Verbs:** For example, humping huge and ungainly loads
- **Adverbs:** For example, ferries plied doggedly

Exercise 2

Now re-read the three passages above; from each one select two or three descriptions and explain carefully how the examples you have chosen use language to achieve their effects. In particular, you should consider the writers' vocabulary, the range and type of sentence structures they use, their tone of voice and the figures of speech they use.

Exercise 3

Here is a rather bland account. Rewrite it, by adding some additional details and information, using descriptive writing tools such as similes, metaphors, adjectives, carefully chosen verbs and adverbs, to create (i) a happy atmosphere and (ii) a threatening atmosphere.

> Anwar was walking beside the river. It was during the afternoon. The day had been hot but now the sun was no longer directly overhead. Anwar had been at school for the whole day. He was feeling tired and wanted to get home quickly. He was thinking about his dinner and seeing his family. Ahead of him he could see some figures. They were coming towards him. The sun's rays made it difficult to see them clearly. He could not recognise any of the figures. They came closer to him. They stopped in front of him and spoke to him.

Warning

Use adjectives and similes sparingly; overuse of them can produce a rather static and overloaded piece of descriptive writing.

Exercise 4

Write a descriptive paragraph giving a clear and precise description of the following; remember to concentrate on describing and not writing a narrative. Try to make your description as interesting as possible:

The family car

A school classroom

An old person riding a bicycle

The view from your bedroom window early in the morning

A busy city street

Preparing for a descriptive writing task

Here is a descriptive writing task and some thoughts of a candidate about how to approach it and what could be included in it. Think about these points and then organise the notes into paragraph topics and write your own essay using them. (You need not include all the points or suggestions.)

Describe a busy local market

Notes

Do I take a narrative approach or should I just focus on giving impressions?

Describe some of the stalls and the people who run them.

Describe some of the customers.

What time of day shall I choose?

What about the weather?

The location of the market.

The senses: sounds, sights, smells (taste and touch?)

Do I describe the market in a positive or negative way?

What is my attitude to the vendors – are they to be trusted?

What tone of voice do I use? Should I be humorous or should I just give a straightforward account?

I must remember the reader. He or she won't be familiar with the market so I must make sure that my details are clear.

Finally, here is a selection of descriptive essay titles similar to those that you will be given in the examination. Choose one and write between 450 and 600 words.

a. Describe somewhere you go to when you want to be alone and say why this place is so special to you.

b. Describe the scene at a concert hall or sports ground before the main event begins.

c. Describe your favourite shop or market stall and some of the people who work there.

d. Describe a ceremony in which all your family took part.

e. Describe a place which you know well at two different times of the day.

Chapter **5**

Argumentative Writing

An argumentative writing task requires you to construct a logically-developed argument. ('To recount views', Assessment Objective i). It is not necessary to attempt to give equal weight to opposing points of view, but what you write should be clear and rational and supported by appropriate examples and references. You should try to avoid becoming too emotional in your approach and/or filling your essay with personal comments and anecdotes which detract from your main line of argument.

Exercise 1

Here is an example of a piece of argumentative writing. Read it through carefully and list the features that you think make it an effective piece of argumentative writing. Do you think that there are any features of it which reduce its effectiveness? Do not read the commentary which follows until you have done this.

> 'You Can't Judge a Book by its Cover.'
>
> Do you agree with this statement?

I often hear people say things like, 'Wow! Look at that girl! I love her dress,' or, 'Oooh, see that boy! He's got a great physique !!' When saying these things, do we ever stop to think that we are only looking at the appearance of a person and not at their inner self and what they possess inside them?

Nowadays, people seem to concentrate too much on what they look like and what others think of them. It always seems to be about a person's appearance and not about that person's actual personality. This is a mistaken attitude to have, as we fail to see what people are really like and what they have inside them.

As humans, we tend to make judgements of people by looking only at their appearance. For instance, people say, 'Look at the dress that girl is wearing! I'm sure she can't come from a very good family.' In saying this, we have automatically judged that girl only on the grounds of what she looks like and the clothes she is wearing. We have failed to see what lies inside her and what she is really like. We do this all the time, often without realising that we are doing it. Is that what we really want?

A number of people may argue that it is a good thing to dress up and look good, not only for others but for ourselves as well. I definitely agree with this. However, it should not happen to the extent that this becomes everything a person cares about. Think about it; if all we cared about was what we looked like, nobody would see us for the people we really are, but rather for what we look like on the outside. If we continue with this attitude then we may well produce a future society which cares only about superficial appearance; is this what we really want? I don't think so.

When watching television we automatically make comments about how good-looking or not certain presenters are and quite often comment on what they are wearing. In many cases, however, while we are doing this we fail to take any notice of what they are saying and the important messages they may be trying to communicate. This is what having too much interest in appearance is doing to us. It makes us miss out on some of the important things we should be paying attention to.

People, often teenagers, say things such as, 'There's no way I'd go out with that girl; she's so unattractive !' Such a comment shows that the person making it has been conditioned by the attitudes of the society of which he is a part. His friends tend to spend their time commenting on the appearance of people, and so he automatically judges the girl only by what she looks like – and the appreciation of beauty is a very subjective thing, anyway. I'm sure this is not the attitude we would want our children to have. We must stop paying too much attention to the physical appearance of people around us, and of ourselves.

Being too interested in appearance even leads to people being distracted from their studies. I'm sure parents have heard their children say things like, 'Mum, I can't study right now. I have to get ready and look good. I'm going out tonight!' This is exactly what happens when people care too much about their appearance. They usually tend to stop doing work only because they care so much about their appearance. It becomes a pointless distraction.

We, as individuals in our society, must make sure that we stop worrying too much about our appearance as this is what will lead to us becoming an egotistic and ignorant generation. Appearance is NOT everything.

This is an essay written under examination conditions and it was rewarded with a good mark. What makes it an effective piece of argumentative writing?

- The tone is confident, not overly formal and clearly conveys the attitude of the writer.

- There is a focused and direct opening which immediately engages the reader.

- The writer keeps the argument within the bounds of his/her own experience.

- There is a clear focus on the topic.

- The writer does not try to include more points than it is possible to handle within the limited time available.

- The essay is structured through logically connected paragraphs which help to further the writer's argument.

- There is a confident control of sentence structures and types with short sentences being used effectively to emphasise key points.

- The writer skilfully blends direct statements with direct questions which engage the reader and develop the argument.

- The essay develops from particular comments to more generalised concerns which widen the scope of the argument.

- There is a strong conclusion which powerfully sums up and re-emphasises the writer's point of view.

Planning Points

A good argumentative essay should be based on a well-controlled structure which leads the reader clearly from a well-defined opening to a forceful conclusion. A good way to make a plan for such an essay is by writing down the topics of each paragraph and then organising them into their most effective order. Here is the paragraph plan for the essay printed above:

- Introduction: Do we judge people only by their appearance? Note that, for effect, the writer has made this point the topic of the opening two paragraphs.

- It is a feature of human nature to do so.

- However, many people consider it important to look good.

- At some time or other we all comment on the appearance of other people.

- Our opinions of people's appearance are influenced by the views of those around us.

- But beauty is in the eye of the beholder.

- Conclusion: appearance is NOT everything and a society which thinks it is will not be a pleasant one.

Exercise 2

Here is a less successful attempt at writing an argumentative essay. This has been reproduced exactly as written and contains many errors of expression. It contains a number of relevant points but the structure of the essay and the linking between paragraphs have quite serious limitations. Read the essay carefully and then (i) re-write it, correcting all the errors of expression that you can identify and (ii) write your own response to the task, using the ideas contained in this essay, but re-organising and developing them to produce a more focused piece of work.

> The title of the essay is: 'Do you consider sport an important part of life?'

Sports means every physical and mental effort we make to use extra energy our body consume, for example energies like fat, that most of us consume regularly. Sport is the key to a healthier life.

Sport is an important part of our life. Through sport we can prevent us from getting diseases like cholesterol, cardiovascular diseases, diabetes. Doing sports activities will help us from getting these diseases. Nowday, campaigns are made by government to sensitise people about diseases like cholesterol, diabetes as this level of people carring diabetes is rising everyday.

With sport, specially football helps us to develop strategies either in playing football or in other part of our life, for example in making new business strategies, in business decision making. And also sports helps us to face problems in life and become more responsible, patient and face social matters more easily and become more dynamic.

Nowdays sport is not only becoming an activity better a job because many people are talent in many sport field like football, Athletics and many others, scientifically in is prove that when a person is doing sport, his/her organs are more developed than those who are not doing. By doing sport the life expectancy of our organs tend to have a longer life than other citizens. Also with sport we help our body to re-inforce our muscles so as to be able to do work which needs efforts and in some ways helping others like encouraging friends or neighbours to do sport, by showing them how to do sports.

By giving elders and youngsters the example that we must do sport to have a good health, encourage future generations to have a good health by doing sports and naturally will sensitise people not only to have a good health but also to a good health we need a good environment, and also a good or clear place to do sports activities. By this it will carry down a reduction in pollution, of course it won't be an immediate change it will take years to come, but where there is a will there is a way.

Sports for me is not only important in some way or another it is vital. Because with sport we can bring many changes in our life either Physical, Health, or Attitudes and behaviours, with sport a *person can be more discipline and responsible in life. Sports is the key to success.*

Exercise 3: Structuring an argument

Here is a collection of jumbled topic sentences which when reorganised will provide the skeleton for an argumentative essay on the subject, 'Life is so easy for teenagers today; it was so much harder when their parents were young.' How far do you agree with this comment? Organise the sentences into what you consider to be the most effective order and then write your essay based on this plan.

- Advances in technology have made things a lot easier for teenagers nowadays.

- When I compare my life with that of my parents I notice that there are many differences.

- On the other hand, my friends and I face considerably more and different pressures.

- Taking all these points into consideration, it is possible to come to the following conclusion.

- Other changes in society have also meant that today's teenagers have an easier time than our parents did.

- These were certainly issues which did not bother our parents as the causes of them did not exist in their day.

Emotive Vocabulary

In Chapter 2, we looked at how carefully chosen vocabulary allows a writer to convey precise shades of meaning. Having an awareness of the connotations associated with certain words and phrases and of their effect on a reader is particularly helpful when you are writing argumentatively and trying to encourage a reader to agree with your point of view. Consider these statements made by a politician:

'We should consider the possibility of raising taxes; however, our opponents in parliament will not be in favour of this.'

'We should consider the possibility of raising taxes; however, our enemies in parliament will not be in favour of this.'

'Opponent' is a neutral word; it simply refers to members of a different political party with different principles. 'Enemies', however, is an emotionally-charged word and implies that the people with different ideas (the same people who were described in the previous sentence as 'opponents') have some malicious purpose and want to cause harm to the speaker and his/her colleagues. The second sentence would be likely, therefore, to provoke an angrier response from the speaker's supporters.

Emotive Language Exercise 4

Identify and explain the effects of the emotively-charged language in the following paragraph:

Out in the vast and empty oceans, if we are lucky, we will be able to observe the whales – the noble, graceful and immensely powerful giants of the sea. They are peaceful creatures whose self-contained, gentle lives do not interfere with our land-based existence. We become aware of them when they burst awesomely from the depths, spouting water skywards as if in greeting to those who are watching. And yet, there are some people whose response to their nobility and innocent joy of living is a harsh and cruel one. To them, the whale is an object of sport which they must hunt and destroy in order to prove the pathetic superiority of their murderous technology. The factory ships are a dark stain on the wide seas.

Tools for argumentative writing

When you are writing to express your views on a particular topic, one of your main concerns is to convince your readers of your point of view and to persuade them to agree with you. There are certain writing techniques that you can use which will help you to be successful in this purpose. For example, with this type of writing, it is important that you adopt an appropriate tone (you should aim to be persuasive but not aggressive); you should pay close attention to the structure of your argument, particularly to introductory and concluding paragraphs and to the devices you use to link paragraphs as a way of furthering your argument. Remember to try to use actual examples and, if appropriate, facts and statistics to support your arguments. You also need to think carefully about your vocabulary, especially whether to choose emotively-toned words.

Exercise 5

Here is an extract from an essay entitled *The Sporting Spirit* by George Orwell. It is a good example of how an argument is constructed and expressed in such a way as to persuade the reader to share the writer's point of view. Read the passage carefully and then, with a partner, make notes of the main points of Orwell's argument and then identify and explain key features of his expression, in particular commenting on any use of emotively-toned language. Read the comments following the passage after you have done this.

I am always amazed when I hear people saying that sport creates goodwill between the nations, and that if only the common people of the world could meet one another at football or cricket, they would have no inclination to meet on the battlefield. Even if one didn't know from concrete examples (the 1936 Olympic Games, for instance) that international sporting contests lead to orgies of hatred, one could deduce it from general principles.

Nearly all the sports practised nowadays are competitive. You play to win, and the game has little meaning unless you do your utmost to win. On the village green where you pick up sides and no feeling of local patriotism is involved, it is possible to play simply for the fun and exercise: but as soon as the question of prestige arises, as soon as you feel that you and some larger unit will be disgraced if you lose, the most savage combative instincts are aroused. Anyone who has played even in a school football match knows this. At the international level sport is frankly mimic warfare. But the significant thing is not the behaviour of the players but the attitude of the spectators: and behind the spectators, of the nations who work themselves into furies over these absurd contests, and seriously believe – at any rate for short periods – that running, jumping and kicking a ball are tests of national virtue.

(Orwell now gives some examples that he has witnessed of the behaviour of spectators at different sporting events in different countries throughout the world before making the following conclusion.)

As soon as strong feelings of rivalry are aroused, the notion of playing the game according to the rules vanishes. People want to see one side on top and the other side humiliated, and they forget that victory gained through cheating or through the intervention of the crowd is meaningless. Even when the spectators don't intervene physically they try to influence the game by cheering their own side and 'rattling' opposing players with boos and insults. Serious sport has nothing to do with fair play. It is bound up with hatred, jealousy, boastfulness, disregard of all rules and sadistic pleasure in witnessing violence: in other words it is war minus the shooting.

Source: 'In front of Your Nose' in *Collected Essays, Journalism and Letters of George Orwell*, Volume 4, Penguin Books

This is a good example of a piece of effective argumentative writing. Orwell adopts a deliberately controversial stance; his tone of voice, however, is initially calm and reasoned, at times almost colloquial in its use of abbreviations ('didn't') and personal pronouns ('you') both of which devices help to directly involve the reader. As well as this, however, Orwell cleverly uses more generalised statements such as 'Nearly all the sports practised nowadays…' and 'People want to see one side on top…' which give his argument a sense of authority. The overall balanced tone of the writing also serves to give greater force to the emotively-toned vocabulary ('orgies of hatred', 'savage combative instincts', 'sadistic pleasure in witnessing violence') which occurs effectively throughout the piece. The writer also skilfully controls his sentence structures using a mixture of complex and shorter sentences to great effect; this technique is used most effectively in the sentence which concludes the extract and which emphatically states the author's point of view.

Exercise 6

Now, using your summary of the main points made by Orwell in *The Sporting Spirit*, write your own essay on the topic in which you present an opposing argument.

Exercise 7

Write an argumentative essay on the topic: *Money Can't Buy Happiness*. How far do you agree with this statement?

Given below, in no particular order, are some comments which you may want to use as points in your argument.

Record amounts are being paid out by parents on birthday parties and celebrations to ensure that their child's big day is one to remember.

Ian Wright, one time professional footballer and now a TV presenter, spent three days in the wilderness with Kalahari Bushmen. 'I feel very humbled by the Bushmen,' he said. 'They don't know anything other than their life and they seem pretty happy.'

'Have you ever added up the cost of bringing up a child? Parents in the UK may spend up to £10,000 a year in bringing up their children.'

A family of three young children and their mother are in mourning for their father who committed suicide when he lost a winning lottery ticket.

City traders can earn millions but their average retirement age has fallen to below 40; stress and sickness are the causes.

More and more people are finding that giving to those in need is more satisfying than buying luxuries for themselves.

Finally, here is a selection of argumentative essay titles similar to those that you will be given in the examination. Choose one and write between 450 and 600 words.

i. 'The challenges of life bring out the best in young people.' What are your views?

ii. 'People are much too interested in their appearance nowadays.' Do you agree?

iii. What aspects of your education do you think will be most useful to you in adult life?

iv. 'Animals and birds should never be kept in cages.' What is your opinion?

v. 'Children do not spend enough time with their parents nowadays.' What is your opinion?

Chapter

Discursive Writing

Assessment Objective (i) states that you should be able to 'recount personal experience, views and feelings'. Sometimes, these requirements are tested individually through descriptive writing tasks (which allow you to recount your feelings) or argumentative tasks (in which you can express your views). Some essay topics, however, allow you a much wider scope as they allow you to refer to all three aspects of the Assessment Objective; such essays are what are known as discursive writing tasks. You have a certain amount of freedom in the way you approach the tasks as you are able to make your own decision about the particular aspect of the task that you want to make the focus of your writing.

Exercise 1

Here is an example of a discursive topic and of a candidate's attempt to answer it. As you read it make notes of what you consider make it an effective piece of writing. Are there any aspects of the essay which are less successful? In particular, you should consider the writer's use of language and the structure of the argument.

MUSIC

William Shakespeare, one of the greatest writers who ever lived, said: 'If music be the food of love, play on.' Isn't that enough testimony to the power of music?

Each one of us listens to music everyday, whether consciously or subconsciously. We hear it everywhere on the radio, on the television, on our compact disc player, and even perhaps, in the next door neighbour's whistling. Be it music from the 60s, pop music, grunge, rap, classical baroque or Mozart symphonies, it is all from the same family — music.

Music has evolved over the centuries. Two or three hundred years ago, everyone was listening to what we now call classical music. This was what made composers like Beethoven, Bach, Haydn and many others famous. Over the last one hundred or so years, a great range of popular music has developed including the music of the Beatles which appealed to our parents in the 60s through to popular rock music of today from which bands such as Chemical Romance and Nickelback are raking in millions of dollars.

Without a doubt, music has a positive effect on the psyche, as proven by studies around the world. Soothing music such as slow ballads or instrumental music calms the senses and helps us to relax. It helps us to unwind after a long day at work and therefore reduces stress levels. Heavy metal and rock music, on the other hand, can also produce a beneficial effect, albeit in a different manner as some people prefer listening to loud music to release tension and stress as they feel that works for them. If it does them good, who are we to tell them to turn the volume down? Studies have also shown that listening to classical music helps with brain development. This is why expectant mothers often put on music by Mozart in the hope that their child will grow up to be the next Einstein.

Music can break down barriers of distance, age, race and creed, as shown by the 'Live 8' concert which was held not too long ago at eight different locations around the world simultaneously. These concerts were held in the hope of raising enough funds to alleviate poverty in the continent of Africa. The project was a success and definitely proved that music can bring people together.

National anthems are also a form of music and, more importantly, they are national symbols for a country. Most champion athletes will say that the greatest moment in their lives is when their national anthem is played as they receive their Olympic or World Championship medals. Indeed, most organisations, including schools, have their own anthems with which their members can identify. These tunes symbolise oneness and unity and are sung by everyone who belongs to that organisation, regardless of their position within it.

However, too much of something is not a good thing. If we have our radio on at full volume throughout the day, seven days a week, sooner or later it could take a toll on our hearing as our hearing range will decrease and in some cases this may result in deafness. Therefore, we should always be sensible about what we do and listen to music in moderation.

Much has been said about music throughout history and, whether we like it or not, it is here to stay. Music allows songwriters to express their feelings through lyrics, pianists to express their emotions through their piano playing and it is a vast industry which provides many people with their daily living. So, why not look through that CD collection of yours, choose a song you like and spin it for, according to Auerbach, 'music washes away the dust of everyday life.'

The writer of this essay has sensibly decided to focus on only a limited range of ideas. (One of the potential problems with one-word titles is that without careful planning it is very easy for a candidate in an examination to try to include too many points and become confused.) This writer has deliberately chosen to write about the type of music which most appeals to him or her but has developed from writing about specific types of music to make some more general comments about the value of music to all people. The essay is well structured and the use of quotations at the beginning and end to act as a kind of frame for the ideas included, is particularly effective.

Tools for Discursive Writing

Planning points

Discursive essay writing requires a different approach from writing an argumentative essay. A successful discursive essay covers a range of points which allows the writer to express his or her own experiences, views and feelings although none of these points is necessarily any more important than another. This means, that very often, a discursive essay does not follow a single line of argument but instead contains a range of points linked by the common theme of the title. For this reason, when planning this type of essay, you may find that a spider diagram approach is the most effective way of doing so. For example, the essay on Music would have had a plan something like this:

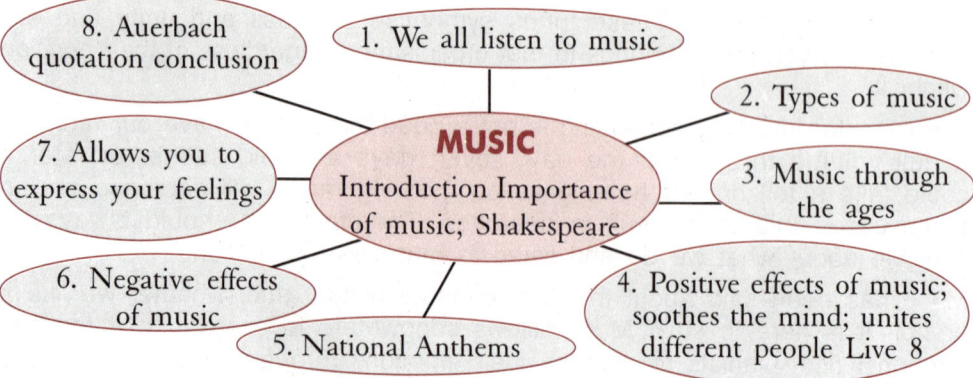

As you can see, there is no correct order in which these ideas can be expressed (apart from the introduction and conclusion); the skill of the writer lies in relating them together within the general framework.

Exercise 2

Perhaps more than in other types of writing, the discursive essay is something in which the style of the writer is as important as the content of the essay. The real skill in producing this type of writing lies in the ability to take a single topic and then elaborate upon it, developing it in a variety of ways through making imaginative connections between different ideas. Here is an example of a professional writer dealing with the apparently uninteresting title 'Appetite'. Read through the essay carefully and when you have finished write two or three paragraphs in which you comment on what makes it an effective piece of discursive writing. You should comment on the writer's use of language, his use of examples and the structure of his writing.

One of the major pleasures in life is appetite, and one of our major duties should be to preserve it. Appetite is the keenness of living; it is one of the senses that tells you that you are still curious to exist, that you still have an edge on your longings and want to bite into the world and taste its multitudinous flavours and juices.

By appetite, of course, I don't mean just the lust for food, but any condition of unsatisfied desire, any burning in the blood that proves you want more than you've got, and that you haven't used up your life. Wilde said he felt sorry for those who never got their heart's desire, but sorrier still for those who did. I got mine once only, and it nearly killed me, and I've always preferred wanting to having since.

For appetite, to me, is this state of wanting, which keeps one's expectations alive. I remember learning this lesson long ago as a child when treats were few, and when I discovered that the greatest pitch of happiness was not in actually eating a toffee but in gazing at it beforehand. True, the first bite was delicious, but once the toffee was gone one was left with nothing, neither toffee nor lust. Besides, the whole toffeeness of toffees was imperceptibly diminished by the gross act of having eaten it. No, the best was in wanting it, in sitting and looking at it, when one tasted an inexhaustible treasure-house of flavours.

So, for me, one of the keenest pleasures of appetite remains in the wanting, not the satisfaction. In wanting a peach, or a lemonade, or a particular texture or sound, or to be with a particular friend. For in this condition, of course,

I know that the object of desire is always at its most flawlessly perfect. Which is why I would carry the preservation of appetite to the extent of deliberate fasting, simply because I think that appetite is too good to lose, too precious to be destroyed completely through over-indulgence.

For that matter, I don't really want three square meals a day — I want one huge, delicious table-groaning feast, say every four days, and then not to be too sure where the next one is coming from. A day of fasting is not for me just a means of denying myself a pleasure, but rather a way of anticipating a rarer moment of supreme indulgence.

Too much of anything — too much music, entertainment, happy snacks or time spent with friends, creates a stupefied state in which one can no longer hear, or taste, or see, or love, or remember. Life is short and precious, and appetite is one of its guardians, and loss of appetite is a sort of death. So if we are to enjoy this short life we should respect the value of appetite, and keep it eager and not too much blunted.

It is a long time now since I knew that acute moment of bliss that comes from putting parched lips to a cup of cold water. The springs are still there to be enjoyed – all one needs is the original thirst.

Source: *I Can't Stay Long* by Laurie Lee, Penguin Books

In this essay Laurie Lee has chosen to base his ideas on his own life experiences and his character and personality are clearly apparent, most noticeably in the third paragraph in which the example of the experience of eating a toffee as a child is developed into a detailed account which, despite its light-hearted tone, nevertheless contains a serious reflection on the nature of human experience.

Exercise 3

This is an essay written on the topic 'What lessons can we learn from the past?' As you will see, the writer has some quite good ideas but fails to make very much of them. Re-write the essay, developing fully the points originally made and adding ideas of your own. You may choose to conclude with a statement different from that of the original writer.

Lessons from the past don't always make our present life happier; sometimes those lessons make our life worse because we can never forget how we learnt those lessons. Parents always tell us that we can learn the hard way or the easy way; the easy way being we listen to them and do what they tell us to, and the hard way being to go out there, do something and actually realise that maybe we should not have done that but now we have learnt our lesson so we won't do it again. People say, 'Once bitten, twice shy'. I believe this is true and I've learnt a lot of my lessons this way such as now I know it's not a good idea to run into a wall because a broken arm and a sprained wrist have made me scared to go anywhere near a solid wall and I know I won't be running into one again soon but I don't think that lesson will make my present life happier because I am just left with memories and an arm I can't put any pressure on.

Some lessons I learnt make my present life happy. I'm glad I never walked off with a stranger as my parents told me not to do, but I don't think the lessons we learnt in the past have much influence on the way we live our present lives.

Exercise 4

Here are some discursive writing topics accompanied by some suggested opening paragraphs. Make your own spider diagram plans for each one of the topics and then write your own essay(s) on one or more of them developing from the given paragraphs.

Weekends

Weekends never seem to arrive and when they do they are over too soon. They are times when the whole family can be together at home to do what they wish. For those of us who are at school they provide an opportunity to catch up with some much needed sleep, to complete those pieces of homework we've been intending to do every night of the week yet somehow never got round to and also, weekends are times for us to relax and spend time with our friends. Weekends provide opportunities for everyone no matter what their age or circumstances.

The Joys of Travel

What is meant by the word 'travel'? To some people it means spending a lot of money and flying to far-away places for a family holiday; to others it could simply involve leaving home in the morning and making the same journey to their place of work or study as they did the day before and the day before that. It depends on your outlook as to whether you see travel as being a functional or romantic activity. Those who think in the former way are likely to see their main means of travel as being either on foot or by using public transport such as buses and trains. On the other hand, those who seek the romance of travel may want to make long sea voyages or dream of riding round the world on a powerful motorcycle and camping under the stars at night. The joys of travel are many and varied.

Food

Food means different things to different people. Basically, it can be defined as substances which we ingest everyday to keep us alive. To some people it is no more than this; to others it is a source of pleasure and excitement and to these people discovering and sampling different kinds of food and recipes from all parts of the world is one of the great motivations of their lives. In contrast to this, however, far too many people in some parts of the world suffer from shortage of food and are unsure as to where their next meal will come from. We need to keep all of these ideas in mind when writing about this topic.

Living in a City

'It's too noisy; I can't hear myself think. Everybody is rushing about with no care for anyone else. All I want to do is to leave this town and retire to the countryside where I can be at peace among the pleasures of nature.'

'There's nothing more exciting than living in the middle of a great city. You have all the entertainment you want – cinemas, theatres, concert halls, sports arenas. Everywhere you look, people are moving around purposefully; it's said that the city never sleeps – I wish that I could be awake 24 hours a day to make the most of what it has to offer.'

These are just two opinions about living in a city; where do your own views fit in?

Finally, here is a selection of discursive essay titles similar to those that you will be given in the examination. Choose one and write between 450 and 600 words.

> Write about some of the things that make you happy and relaxed at the end of a school day
>
> Cats
>
> Being Young
>
> Mistakes and Misunderstandings
>
> The Future is a Serious Matter

Chapter **7**

Personal Writing

Sometimes the assessment objective to 'recount personal experience' is tested directly by essay titles which require you to write about an experience or occasion that has occurred in your own life. If you decide to tackle such a task, it is worth keeping some guidelines in mind.

- It is better to base what you write on something which actually happened rather than trying to invent a situation and claiming it is true.

- The reader, however, will not know what really happened so you can elaborate a little on the details or even combine two actual separate experiences into one.

- The reader will not know anything about your personal circumstances so remember that you need to provide a context to your account and to give some brief information about other people who were involved.

- Remember you are at the centre of the piece of writing – it is important that you make yourself interesting and communicate the key elements of your personality.

Exercise 1

Here is an example of a piece of personal writing; the author is writing about an unusual sporting contest which she witnessed while visiting an island in the Caribbean. Read it carefully and then make a list of the features which make it an effective piece of personal writing. In particular comment on how well it fulfils the rules printed above.

Crab Racing

Crab racing turned out to be an inspiration. I don't know how long it had been since the creatures left their natural habitat but they looked as if they had resigned themselves to their fate. Even if the barrel they had just been taken from contained sea water or, alternatively, mud from their very own

swamp, all memory of home had now gone. They languished in the afternoon sun as if they hadn't a care in the world. Since ropes would be ridiculous on creatures that size, a sturdy piece of string was attached to the anatomy of each crustacean. The minders spent much time in examining claws and paying attention to details. In addition to the string, there was a second prop. It was one which could be described as the urging and steering mechanism—a stick. When the race began I tried not to rationalize or demand too much logic from what was taking place. But it was madness to the utmost degree. A number of male adults were holding a piece of string. At the other end of the string was a crab. The men were endeavouring to urge the creatures forward at a satisfactory pace with the aid of the stick. One crab was going backwards and continued to do so regardless of any attempts to the contrary. Three of them appeared to be moving diagonally. Two others seemed to be dancing a quadrille.

As always, there was a maverick. Slowly but surely he was inching forward. The crab was moving slowly but surely towards the finishing line. It was not so much a race as an exercise in patience. Not far removed from taking your pet snail for a walk. There was no longer any reason to scuttle. When you scuttle, you move with some intent to escape. If you are tethered by a string and the radius of your movement is governed by its length, then what's the point? These crustaceans, in any case, looked as if they no longer knew the meaning of the word scuttle. Even worse, some seemed to be experiencing difficulty in moving a claw forward. I didn't know the rules of the race. Were there any? Was it my imagination or did I notice some tugging on the string? It would obviously serve to pull the crab forward at a speed not of its own volition. My eyes were riveted on the maverick some short distance from the finishing line.

The spectators were better behaved than the ones in Trinidad. However, one or two began voicing their doubts about the precise physical condition of the winner.

'You damn cheat!'

'The crab dead! All you can't see the crab dead?!!'

I felt the protestors had a point. The only movement from the crab was the involuntary one made by any motion of the string.

'How all you people so blasted stupid? All you can't see the crab already dead when he haul it across the line?!'

> This was very interesting. The crab went into a series of jerks as the minder worked the string to demonstrate it was still in the land of the living. Alternatively, it could indeed have been involuntary. Death throes.
>
> 'How man in he right mind go want pin medal on dead crab?!'
>
> Howls of laughter from the spectators. The winner sat unconcerned. Surely rigor mortis had now set in. At any rate, no attempt was being made to lift a claw in triumphant acclamation of victory.
>
> 'And I say it dead before it cross the line!'
>
> A number of people formed a circle around the winner. There was much close inspection going on.
>
> 'He move! I see he move!' It was confirmed by another person in the circle. There was much jubilation. Everyone seemed happy. Everyone, that is, except the crab. And while we settled down to enjoy the rest of the afternoon, I was left with my doubts. Was there life in that body when the first claw slithered across the line?
>
> Source: *Sequins for a Ragged Hem* by Amryl Johnson in Travel Wnting, Oxford Literature Resources

Here, the writer has chosen to describe her experience of an unusual event – crab racing. She skilfully captures the atmosphere of the occasion, in particular through her reproduction of the speech of the other spectators. However, what makes this a particularly effective account is the personality of the writer: she comes across as being fascinated, amused and a little bewildered and the informal tone she uses, reinforced by some direct questions successfully engages the reader.

Exercise 2

The following example of a piece of personal writing was written under examination conditions. It was awarded quite a good mark but, as you will notice when you read it, its structure, expression and the writer's focus on the topic could be improved. The title is: *Write about two occasions when you had great fun as a child*.

> Everybody has <u>a lot of memories to remember</u>, especially those during childhood. Whether they are sweet or bad memories they remain fresh in our minds. People always say that sweet memories are hard to forget. I really agree with this statement because we cannot deny it. Memories will always remain. I want to share with you two occasions when I had great fun as a young child. The first is of when I entered primary school and

the second is when my family celebrated my birthday without my knowing.

1994 was when I entered primary school. When my father drove me to Sunnyside Primary School I felt very scared because I did not know my new situation and environment. When we arrived at that school, my feelings changed from scared to excited because the environment of the school was very beautiful. It was surrounded by many plants and a few metres away from the school could be seen a beach. The beach is known as Golden Sands Beach.

When I entered the class, I saw many children with their own parents. Some of them were happy because they were going to meet new friends but others were crying. My mother always gave me support and encouraged me not to be scared but to be happy at all times. Moreover, my cousins were in the same class as me. I would soon be making new friends.

As the time passed by, we all got to know each other well and played together. It was a good time when I made new friends. Although I am seventeen now, it is hard to forget them because they were all kind and always helpful to me especially if I had any difficulties in a particular subject.

My second occasion when I had great fun as a young child was during the celebrations for my seventh birthday. One day before my birthday came, that is on the 4th April 1996, it seemed strange that my parents did not bring me and my brothers and sisters to go shopping because usually before a birthday they would bring us to buy stationery and new clothes.

My parents went shopping by themselves and when they got home, as usual, they had bought household goods and new stationery for my brothers and sisters. However, I felt very sad because they said that they had forgotten to buy new clothes and stationery for me. Because of my parents' lack of concern, I cried alone in my room.

Later, on the morning of April 5th 1996 as usual my brothers and sisters and I went to school and when we came back home, I was surprised because my parents celebrated my birthday party and had bought me a chocolate cake. I felt very happy when my parents gave me a big present that was a bicycle and then held me tightly.

Those are two occasions that were very exciting and fun. I will never forget either of them. They will always be in my mind.

This writer of this essay adopts a logical narrative approach to the topic. The content is relevant and gives a clear account of two separate occasions (although the description of the birthday celebrations tends to concentrate more on feelings of sadness than fun). However, the account is a little lacking in excitement and interest; the character of the writer is not clearly apparent as although he makes an attempt to state his feelings he does not explore them in any great detail. Similarly, although the written expression is largely accurate, the vocabulary and sentence structures are a little repetitive and lacking in originality: these are further reasons why the writer's personality is not communicated strongly.

Some words and phrases in the essay have been underlined as more suitable expressions could be put in their place. Rewrite these passages, using words of your own, in order to make the account more interesting or to correct an error of expression.

Exercise 3

Write about your own first day at school (either at primary or secondary school). In particular, concentrate on describing particular details of the day which remain in your memory and try to bring out the feelings you had about the experience – be honest in your description; the feelings can be happy or sad.

Tools for Personal Writing

The key to effective personal writing lies in (i) the selection and treatment of a suitable episode (or episodes) to describe and (ii) the way you present yourself as narrator.

Exam questions that ask for a piece of personal writing will usually suggest that you write about a specific occasion in your life, for example. Describe an occasion when you tried to be helpful but things went wrong. It is important that you focus what you write closely on what the question requires and avoid producing a mini-autobiography of your life up to that point. You do not have time to attempt to describe too complicated an event when writing under examination conditions. However, when thinking about approaching a personal writing task such as the one above, once you have decided on the episode about which you plan to write, you will need to make certain decisions; for example:

- What shall I write about?
- How do I describe the event? Will I describe it exactly in the order it

happened, or should I start from the disastrous conclusion and work back to the beginning?

- How much information do I need to give to provide the context for the episode?

- How will I conclude the account? Should I stop at the point when things went wrong or should I finish with a reflection saying what I learned from the experience?

- How much space should I give to describing what other people said and did?

- Should I treat the episode as comic or serious?

- If I decide to be humorous, how can I make it funny for the reader?

All of these are the sort of questions any thoughtful writer is likely to ask before beginning to write. There are, of course, no right or wrong answers. What is important is that you, as a writer, should have thought of these (or similar points) and used them to ensure that whatever approach you take will provide an account which is consistent and convincing.

Humour

Personal essay topics frequently allow the opportunity for writers to approach the account of their chosen episode in a humorous way. It is perfectly acceptable to take such an approach when writing an examination essay but try to avoid being too heavy-handed in trying to communicate what you think might be funny. It is likely that the events described are amusing in themselves – the most effective comic writing comes from the style of the writer and the language in which they are described: very often an understated approach is the most effective. The humour achieved by writers is very much dependent on the way they present their personalities as part of their narrative.

Exercise 4

Here are some answers to the questions posed above: write your own essay based on them.

- I'll describe the time I tried to cook the dinner and nearly set the house on fire.

- Perhaps I could start at the end with an opening sentence such as 'Never again,' I thought as I gazed at the smoke-filled chaos which had once been mother's beloved kitchen.

- I'd better give a bit of background: how old I was; why I thought it would be a good idea to help out with the cooking. I did it as a surprise for Mum and Dad who were out at work. My elder sister was looking after me but she was on the phone with her friends.

- I think the approach I'm taking will allow me to make a reflective conclusion – things wouldn't have gone wrong if I hadn't left everything cooking in the kitchen to watch my favourite TV programme. Perhaps I could finish with my sister being blamed for the whole episode as she wasn't keeping her eye on me!

- I think I'll keep what other people said and did to the minimum – that will give greater emphasis to what Mum and Dad said when they saw what had happened.

- I think humour will provide the best approach. I need to concentrate on describing the things that went wrong in preparing the meal (upsetting bowls of flour etc) as well as the final disaster. The most effective approach will be to present myself as well meaning and naïve and not really understanding how I finished up producing so much chaos.

Reading for Enjoyment

Here is an example of a piece of humorous personal writing. It is taken from Gerald Durrell's autobiography *My Family and Other Animals*. Durrell became a famous naturalist and in this book he describes how his interest in living creatures was formed in his childhood on the Greek island of Corfu. In this episode he describes how he unwittingly caused chaos at lunchtime by leaving a matchbox containing a mother scorpion and her babies on the mantelpiece. The other characters in this account are his mother; his brothers Larry and Leslie; his sister Margo; the family maid Lugaretzia and Gerald's dog, Roger. Much of the humour derives from the way in which the author builds disaster on top of disaster and describes it using an understated narrative voice. This is a very effective piece of humorous, personal writing; as you read it, consider closely how the different aspects of the passage combine to produce an overall description of chaos and confusion.

Lunch-time with Scorpions

Then one day I found a fat female scorpion in the wall, wearing what at first glance appeared to be a pale fawn fur coat. Closer inspection proved that this strange garment was made up of a mass of tiny babies clinging to the mother's back. I was enraptured by this family, and I made up my mind to smuggle them into the house and up to my bedroom so that I might keep them and watch them grow up. With infinite care I manoeuvred the mother and family into a matchbox, and then hurried to the villa. It was rather unfortunate that just as I entered the door lunch should be served; however, I placed the matchbox carefully on the mantelpiece in the drawing-room, so that the scorpions should get plenty of air, and made my way to the dining-room and joined the family for the meal. Dawdling over my food, feeding Roger surreptitiously under the table and listening to the family arguing, I completely forgot about my exciting new captures. At last Larry, having finished, fetched the cigarettes from the drawing-room, and lying back in his chair he put one in his mouth and picked up the matchbox he had brought. Oblivious of my impending doom I watched him interestedly as, still talking glibly, he opened the matchbox.

Now I maintain to this day that the female scorpion meant no harm. She was agitated and a trifle annoyed at being shut up in a matchbox for so long, and so she seized the first opportunity to escape. She hoisted herself out of the box with great rapidity, her babies clinging on desperately, and scuttled on to the back of Larry's hand. There, not quite certain what to do next, she paused, her sting curved up at the ready. Larry, feeling the movement of her claws, glanced down to see what it was, and from that moment things got increasingly confused.

He uttered a roar of fright that made Lugaretzia drop a plate and brought Roger out from beneath the table, barking wildly. With a flick of his hand Larry sent the unfortunate scorpion flying down the table, and she landed midway between Margo and Leslie, scattering babies like confetti as she thumped on the cloth. Thoroughly enraged at this treatment, the creature sped towards Leslie, her sting quivering with emotion. Leslie leapt to his feet, overturning his chair, and flicked out desperately with his napkin, sending the scorpion rolling across

the cloth towards Margo, who promptly let out a scream that any railway engine would have been proud to produce. Mother, completely bewildered by this sudden and rapid change from peace to chaos, put on her glasses and peered down the table to see what was causing the pandemonium, and at that moment Margo, in a vain attempt to stop the scorpion's advance, hurled a glass of water at it. The shower missed the animal completely, but successfully drenched Mother, who, not being able to stand cold water, promptly lost her breath and sat gasping at the end of the table, unable even to protest. The scorpion had now gone to ground under Leslie's plate, while her babies swarmed wildly all over the table. Roger, mystified by the panic, but determined to do his share, ran round and round the room, barking hysterically.

'It's that boy again ...' bellowed Larry.

'Look out! Look out! They're coming!' screamed Margo.

'All we need is a book,' roared Leslie; 'don't panic, hit 'em with a book.'

'What on earth's the matter with you all?' Mother kept imploring, mopping her glasses.

'It's that boy ... he'll kill the lot of us... . Look at the table ... knee-deep in scorpions ... ."

Quick ... quick ... do something ...

Look out, look out I'

'Stop screeching and get a book, for God's sake ... . You're worse than the dog ... . Shut up, Roger.

'By the Grace of God I wasn't bitten ... .'

'Look out ... there's another one ... . Quick ... quick.

'Oh, shut up and get me a book or something.

'But how did the scorpions get on the table, dear ?'

"That boy ... . Every matchbox in the house is a deathtrap ...'

'Look out, it's coming towards me .... Quick, quick, do something ...'

'Hit it with your knife ... your knife ... . Go on, hit it ...'

Since no one had bothered to explain things to him, Roger was under the mistaken impression that the family were being attacked, and that it was his duty to defend them. As Lugaretzia was the only stranger in the room, he came to the logical conclusion that she must be the responsible party, so he bit her in the ankle. This did not help matters very much.

By the time a certain amount of order had been restored, all the baby scorpions had hidden themselves under various plates and bits of cutlery. Eventually, after impassioned pleas on my part, backed up by Mother, Leslie's suggestion that the whole lot be slaughtered was quashed. While the family, still simmering with rage and fright, retired to the drawing-room, I spent half an hour rounding up the babies, picking them up in a teaspoon, and returning them to their mother's back. Then I carried them outside on a saucer and, with the utmost reluctance, released them on the garden wall. Roger and I went and spent the afternoon on the hillside, for I felt it would be prudent to allow the family to have a siesta before seeing them again.

Source: *My Family and other Animals* by Gerald Durrel, Penguin Books

Finally, here is a selection of personal essay titles similar to those that you will be given in the examination.

Choose one and write between 450 and 600 words.

i. Write about some of the things that make you happy and relaxed at the end of a school day.

ii. What changes have you seen in your school since you joined it?

iii. Describe the biggest challenge in your life.

iv. Describe a day when you were very unhappy.

v. Describe a special family celebration when things went unexpectedly wrong.

Chapter **8**

Narrative Writing

Some examination essay topics require you to write a short story. Choosing one of these topics allows you to use your imagination and to show how creative you can be. However, a narrative essay is not an easy option to do well. Before starting on it, you need to consider the following issues:

- Do not make the story too complicated; you have only a limited time and it is important that you plan your answer carefully to keep it tightly focused.

- Keep closely to the given title or topic; too many short stories written under examination conditions lose marks because they wander away from the topic and lose credibility.

- Try to write a story which contains events which could be within your own experience; examiners do not find unsophisticated secret agent stories particularly enjoyable or convincing.

- Try to break up long sections of narrative with passages of direct speech. Remember, however, that making direct speech sound authentic and punctuating it correctly are difficult skills. If you don't get it right your story will not be successful.

- Do not repeat a story you have read or written elsewhere – memorised stories seldom fit the given topic and examiners will always spot the joins.

Exercise 1

Here are two examples of essays written under examination conditions. The topic was to continue the story using the following opening sentences: *Having reluctantly agreed to meet them at 11 pm precisely in this deserted part of town, I anxiously scanned every moving shadow. I was afraid I would miss them, afraid also that they would not turn up.* Both essays deal with a similar topic.

Read through the two stories carefully and make notes of the good and less good qualities contained in each one. Discuss with a partner how they could be improved and which one you think is better and why. Copying out and using the following grid will help you in making this comparison. (The features listed in the grid should also provide a good checklist of points to cover when you are writing your own essays of all types.)

	Essay 1	Essay 2
TREATMENT OF TASK		
Presentation of situation		
Narrative standpoint		
Tone/register		
Vocabulary/expression		
STRUCTURE		
Development of ideas		
Conclusion		
Structure of paragraphs		
Paragraph linking		
TECHNICAL ACCURACY		
Sentence structures: range/variety		
Punctuation		
Grammatical accuracy		
Use of idiom (see page 73)		
Spelling		

Essay 1

Having reluctantly agreed to meet them at 11 pm precisely in this deserted part of town, I anxiously scanned every moving shadow. I was afraid I would miss them, afraid also that they would not turn up.

I hadn't spent this much time alone in so long, it felt wrong. It felt like somehow I wasn't meant to be here. 'Shut up!' I said to myself. 'Don't be stupid.'

As my eyes eventually adjusted to the darkness, objects around me became clearer, much easier to distinguish. I was standing under a huge oak tree, where we had agreed to meet. I knew this must be the right one: there wasn't another tree for miles.

Eventually after what seemed like an age, I heard voices and they seemed to be getting closer. Not yet being able to make out what the voices belonged to, I strained my ears to hear what they were saying.

'No, I'll grab him and you can knock him out.' A cold fear rushed through my veins, I knew for sure that voice belonged to Rajeev. I felt sick to my stomach when I realised that this had all been a plan, Rajeev had it in for me – big time.

I knew in that moment that I had to get away. I had to run. I ran until my heart was pounding my ears and my breath ached in my chest. I ran through fields, over fences and stone walls. I ran through gardens and dark alleyways. I ran along roads and streets that I had never seen before.

When I finally came to a stop, my legs didn't feel like they belonged to me anymore. I looked around and then it hit me. I didn't have a clue where I was. All I had thought about was running and getting as far away from Rajeev as was possible.

I tried to think back to when I was running. I could remember running but my surroundings were hazy. I wasn't even sure if I was in the same town anymore. I sat down on the cold, muddy floor, rested my back against a low wall and closed my eyes.

And then I felt it, a strangled sob, fighting to escape from the pit of my stomach. I had to hold it in, I couldn't cry now. What if someone walks past? I reopened my eyes and blinked to settle the tears. I knew that I wasn't upset about being lost. Well not upset enough to cry anyway. It was Rajeev that bothered me. Now that he had his own little gang, he had become worse than ever. It wasn't just name calling and joking anymore.

Tomorrow was Monday; there was no way I could go back to school. I had to stay away for as long as possible. Wait for things to calm down a bit. I couldn't go back home, I'd be made to go to school. I could sleep here. It was cold and it was muddy but if it meant that I didn't have to go to school tomorrow I was willing to. I curled up in a ball, pulling my knees up to my chest and closed my eyes. I promised myself that by the end of tomorrow I would have everything sorted out. There was just one question left – How?

Essay 2

Having reluctantly agreed to meet them at 11 pm precisely in this deserted part of town, I anxiously scanned every moving shadow. I was afraid I would miss them, afraid also that they would not turn up.

I then hear a crowd of voices, I look around but see nothing, the suspence is killing me.

After 5 months of being bullied, threatened, intimidated, it all comes down to today, this is my chance to show them that they can't do this to me anymore, I've had enough.

I then hear my name being called. 'Where are you?' They shouted.

Next thing there I am standing on my own, with a crowd of 7 boys walking towards me.

I told him to come on his own, but he was obviously too much of a coward, he had to bring his friends.

As they walk towards me, I hear loud footsteps, my heart begins to beat faster and faster.

I have to stay cool and calm. I'm not going to continue to be picked on all the time, I have to be strong.

As the boys are getting closer and closer to me, I'm very scared but I'm not going to show it, otherwise he'll see, and think his won and he can carry on bullying me, and other people, well, he cant, not anymore. It was 11:15 p.m., pitch black, with only the streetlights on, I can honestly say this is the scaryist time in my life.

I then feel a hand over my mouth, then tape goes over it and a bag is placed over my head …

You will almost certainly have come to the conclusion that Essay 1 is the better of the two and your notes in the grid should provide a clear indication as to why. However, both essays share some positive qualities. Both deal with events which are convincingly within the experience of the narrator; neither of them is over-ambitious as each concentrates on one particular episode and develops it effectively without introducing too many complicated twists and turns. Also, each of them appears to have planned for the essay to conclude at a particular point in order to leave the reader in some suspense.

Now we will look at the points in the grid in more detail to see how they can be used to help you in planning your own narrative writing.

TREATMENT OF TASK

- **Presentation of situation and setting**

  The essential point about producing an effective short narrative is to be economical in the telling of the story. Lengthy scene-setting and description is better suited to a long novel. Your concern is to engage your reader as quickly as you can but also to ensure that the situation you are presenting can be understood straightaway. Before starting to write your story, you should try to put yourself in the position of your readers. Ask yourself a couple of straightforward questions such as, "What do my readers need to know?" "What important details about the setting of the story do I need to give them so that they can quickly understand the background of where the events happen?" Remember: you may have a clear idea of the scene in your mind, but a reader will not have unless you give a clear, but not over-detailed, description of it.

- **Narrative standpoint**

  The first decision you have to make is whether you intend to present your story through a first or third person narrative. A first person narrative is possibly more effective in allowing a reader to identify with the narrator (which is particularly important for a short narrative) and it also means that the events described can only be those within the narrator's experience – again, an effective way to limit the focus and range of your narrative. On the other hand, using a third person narrative allows for a more omniscient approach. If you intend your story to conclude with, for example, the death of the central character, then a first person narrative standpoint may present problems!

- **Characters**

  When you are writing a short story (especially under examination conditions), you should try to be as economical as you can in your description of characters and not to include too many of them in your story. It is important that you give some brief and pertinent details about your characters so that your readers can form an idea of them in their minds and can, therefore, build up an understanding of how those characters are likely to act and behave in the course of the story. However, these introductory details need be little more than one sentence character summaries such as, "Rita, who was always on time for everything and never looked untidy or tired" or "Dravid was the sort of person who never panicked and was always a reliable friend." Once you have established your characters, it is important that they then behave consistently with the character you have created for them. (The extract from *My Family and Other Animals* in the chapter on Personal Writing and the short story 'Terror of the Curse' which concludes this chapter are both very good examples of economical presentation of characters and setting.)

- **Tone/register**

The tone and register you use will, to some extent, depend upon the narrative standpoint you have chosen. A first person narrative allows for a more informal, colloquial approach which is suited particularly to the type of story told in the two examples above. The narrator's tone of voice is an effective way of communicating his or her personality and character. A short narrative can be made much more effective if a person's character is communicated through their language register rather than by a lengthy description of that character.

- **Vocabulary/expression**

The vocabulary used by the narrator of the story and his or her sentence patterns are also an effective way of establishing character. An awareness of the associations and connotations of the vocabulary you use will also help to establish a suitable atmosphere for the story you are telling.

Structure

- **Development of ideas**

Your narrative should quickly establish the direction it is going to take and the sequence of events should be planned to develop coherently. Keep your readers in mind at all times; if they find it difficult to follow what is happening, they will quickly lose interest.

- **Conclusion**

When you plan your narrative be sure that you have a clear understanding of how it is going to conclude. You may decide that your final paragraph will wrap up all the loose ends of your story or you may want to leave your readers in mid-air. What is important, however, is that, whatever the ending you choose, it should be the one you have planned for. The best narratives arrive at a logical conclusion, rather than just stopping because the author can think of no more to write. (The logically planned conclusion can, of course, be unexpected by the reader.)

- **Structure of paragraphs**

  You should use paragraphs to structure your story and their topic sentences are likely to provide the key stages of your narrative. Remember; each paragraph should be a unity within itself, but should also contribute to the overall unity of the story you are writing. Although short, one or two sentence paragraphs can be very effective to emphasise details they should be used sparingly; too many short paragraphs result in a fragmented narrative.

- **Paragraph linking**

  Although it is important to link your paragraphs to form a coherent narrative it is equally important that you vary the ways in which you link them to ensure that you retain the interest of your readers. Try to vary the position of the topic sentences as well to add variety to your style.

Technical Accuracy

- **Sentence structures: range/variety**

  Just as you are concerned about varying your paragraph links and lengths, so you should also think about varying the length and structure of the sentences in your narrative. Repetitive sentence types (for example, having all sentences follow the same subject – verb opening pattern: 'It was…', 'He did…', 'She said…') very soon become monotonous. Think about varying word order and mixing simple and complex sentences and use each type as appropriate. For example, the former can effectively create pace in your narrative while the latter are more suitable for reflective or descriptive sections.

- **Use of idiom**

  One of the Assessment Objectives for the examination is that you should be able to write accurately using Standard English. Although narrative writing sometimes requires a less formal tone than some other types of essay, it is important that you still use Standard English – although, if some of the characters in your story speak using a local dialect it is perfectly acceptable to reproduce that at times to add authenticity to your narrative as long as this is not overdone. However, if you are writing in an informal register inappropriate or outdated colloquialisms do not convince your readers of the credibility of the character using them.

- **Punctuation; grammatical accuracy; spelling**

  As in all examination essays, it is important that you observe the conventions of correct spelling, grammar and punctuation. You may, of course, make one of the characters in your story speak ungrammatically for effect but it is important that you show that you can write accurately in the rest of the narrative so that the reader is aware that you are including the ungrammatical sections deliberately to create an intended effect.

Exercise 2

Choose three of the following topics:(a) produce a skeleton plan (using paragraph topic sentences) for each of them. (b) Write opening and concluding paragraphs for each one you have chosen using a first person narrator. (c) Write opening and concluding paragraphs for each one you have chosen using a third person narrator.

  i.   The Closed Door
  ii. Write a story beginning, 'It was just an ordinary weekday morning…'
  iii. Breaking the Rules
  iv. The woman with the bicycle
  v.   Write a story containing the words, 'I knew that it would never work.'

Exercise 3

Here is a short story by the African writer, Mabel Segun. Read it for pleasure in your groups, but while doing so, discuss with each other and make notes about how the author has presented her characters through what they say and what they think and how she has structured the story to produce the twist at the end. You should also consider the tone of the narrator and how this helps to create a humorous effect. When you have collated your comments, independently write your own analysis of the story, explaining what makes this an effective short story.

Terror of the Curse

'The bride is going to die soon.' The voice was not loud, but there was a sudden lull in the music. I looked towards a group of women under the red canopy but could not discover which of them had spoken. They were a typical Lagos group, colourfully dressed with two or three layers of gold chains and coral beads round their necks and curving over their ample bosoms.

'You see,' the voice continued – it was the sort of half-gloating voice our women use when they spread bad news — I now knew which of them had spoken. She was a young woman, very dark, with very smooth skin. Her oval face wore a lively look and the bangles of her wrists jingled like tiny bells as she waved her hands about. 'You see, the bridegroom fell from his mother's back when he was a baby. And they say '— I could hear the ghoulish delight in her voice — 'they say a person like that will have seven wives and they will all die.'

There were excited murmurs from the other women.

'Now, this man, you see ...' the voice continued, but the band suddenly blared forth and the rest was drowned in the noise.

There was a touch on my shoulder and I turned to find the bridegroom behind me. The women had had their backs to the house and had not seen him approaching.

'Did you hear what she said?' he asked and his voice was agitated.

Ayodole and I had been friends from childhood. We first met at a public water pump where we had a fight. It was a jolly good fight — he went home with a swollen eye and I got a bleeding nose — and as most good fights do, ours ended in friendship. So I know him thoroughly. It was unfortunate that he should have such a dread of what he called 'evil forces'. His grandfather was an Ifa priest and from him he had learnt about traditional taboos. He was a Christian and he read his Bible regularly. His fear of demons and sorcerers was no less than his fear of the traditional 'evil forces'.

'Who said?' I temporised, trying to find words to soothe him.

'One of the women. Didn't you hear her?'

'I didn't', I lied.

'She said I fell from my mother's back.'

'Yes?'

'And so my wife's going to die.'

'Nonsense.'

'And six other wives too.'

'More nonsense still. Don't you listen to such stupid talk. I shouldn't worry if I were you. Why, what should kill Aduke? She's the picture of health.'

'Childbirth, for example, or ...'

'Or what?'

'Or ... or ... or T.B.,' he ended lamely.

'Don't you see how silly it all is? Why, there's Aduke coming out with the women of the house. Does she look as if she had T.B? In any case, people don't die of tuberculosis these days.'

Ayodele shook his head. Aduke, a big-boned woman of average height, came out and the guests let out a shout. She was dressed in an expensive damask outfit. Under the huge 'gele' on her head, her large eyes shone with a happiness which in modesty she tried to conceal. She planted a pound note on the forehead of the head drummer, and started dancing; other girls in her age group joined her.

'Where's the bridegroom?' The bride's father asked.

I pushed Ayodele forward and he joined his wife. His male friends followed suit. Soon afterwards he took his bride home.

I gave no further thought to Ayodele's fears till three months later when he rushed into my house looking worried.

'What's the matter?' I asked.

'It's Aduke,' he said.

'Well?'

'I don't know what's wrong with her? I think she's dying.'

'What makes you think so?'

'Well, you see, she's so listless and tires very easily and yesterday she fainted in the kitchen.'

'Has she seen a doctor?' I asked.

'I suggested it and she said it wasn't necessary as she was now all right. I think she's seriously ill and is trying to hide it from me.'

I burst into laughter.

'Silly idiot,' I said, 'your wife is expecting a baby!'

'Do you think so?'

'I am quite certain.'

His face became radiant with pleasure.

I might have known it wouldn't last. As time went on and Aduke grew bigger, Ayodele began to panic.

'Suppose she were to die?'

I told him thousands of women had babies every year.

'Some of them die.'

'Very few nowadays,' I said, 'and your wife needn't be one of them.'

But he would not be comforted. The

night his wife was confined he came to me.

'I couldn't stay at home,' he said and slumped into a chair.

'Suppose they want you - to tell you the news, I mean.'

'I've told them to come for me here.'

I got out some records and played some music.

'Have you had dinner?' I asked.

'I didn't want any,' he said.

I asked my houseboy to bring him some food. He pecked at it until the fork fell to the floor. After that he gave up trying to eat. Each time there was a knock on the door he jumped up. Then he took to pacing up and down the room.

'Look,' I said, and he halted opposite me.

'Sit down.'

He sat down.

'I hope you won't mind my asking, but are you frightfully in love with your wife?'

I had to ask the question for his wife had been obtained for him by his parents and he hadn't seen her till the day before his marriage.

'In love?' he answered, 'certainly not.'

'Then why, ...?' I made a gesture with my pipe.

'It's not Aduke I'm worried about. Can't you see that if she should die it proves the curse is on me? Imagine, one, two, three, seven wives must die before I can be happy. Oh God!'

He put his head on his hands. He was in this attitude when the knock came.

Perhaps he did not hear it for he did not move. I opened the door. A little boy nearly fell into the room.

'Is brother Ayo here?' he asked.

'Anything wrong?' I asked.

He looked past me and saw his brother. He went towards him and said, 'Brother, brother, auntie told me to tell you sister has delivered.'

He jumped up at once.

'What is it?' he asked, his eyes boring into the boy's.

'A boy.'

He turned to me excitedly. 'Did you hear what he said? A boy!'

'So you see ...'I said meaningly. And once again death was averted.

Ayodele seemed to be preoccupied with his child and for a long time I heard no more about the curse.

Then a cholera epidemic broke out in the town. It raged as it had never done before. The hospitals were filled, the babalawos were kept busy working charms, and vaccinators were to be seen in Government Health Centres jabbing needles into people. Ayodele was quite convinced that the cholera outbreak had been sent by some malignant fate purposely to slay his wife.

'But, my dear Ayo,' I said, 'Surely that's a bit too much.'

And then he caught it. He sent his wife and the child away to his parents and his sister stayed on to take care of him. I visited him several times in hospital.

'I hope this has convinced you there's no malignant fate pursuing your wife,' I said.

He gave a sickly smile.

'She hasn't escaped yet. The cholera is still raging.'

Soon he got well, but insisted his wife should stay on with his parents for a little longer. He enjoyed reading his wife's letters even in the semi-literate handwriting. Once, he told me, 'My wife wants to stay on longer with my parents. She says they get on quite well. My parents too say they like her very much. She's so cheerful and everybody likes her. I'm glad she gets on so well with them. It doesn't do to have a wife not liked by one's parents. It brings trouble.'

Once when I visited him he asked me to post a letter for him. I was just going away with it when he asked for it back. He took his pen and, taking the letter out of the envelope, inserted a postcript. I couldn't help seeing it.

'Any cholera in the village yet?' he wrote, then put the letter in another envelope and addressed it.

I smiled and took the letter from him.

One day, he invited me to lunch. I called at his office and we both went to his house. There we found his mother and two other female relatives waiting. There was an air of mourning about them. They sat slumped forward on the mat and greeted us sadly. A little boy gurgled at us from where he sat in front of Ayodele's mother. Filled with apprehension, Ayodele rushed towards them.

'What's wrong?' he asked, his hands shaking.

His mother burst into tears and the two relatives followed suit.

'What is it?' Ayodele repeated. 'Is it about Aduke?' he gulped.

His mother nodded. 'It's not really our fault. I didn't think there was anything wrong at first and when I knew I didn't dare tell you. We tried our best, your father and I ...'

'Is she- dead?' Ayodele asked in despair.

'Dead? No. It's worse. She's run away with a businessman. They're now in London.'

The three women looked at him with anxiety. His mother was shaking her head sorrowfully and the other women were fidgetting with their shawls.

'Is that all, Mother?' Ayodele burst into laughter. He turned to me, 'Let's go and eat,' he said and called out to the houseboy, 'Telemi, make some amala for my mothers.'

There was no curse after all.

Source: *The Surrender and Other Stories* by Mabel Segun, Addition Wesley Publishing Company

Finally, here is a selection of narrative essay titles similar to those that you will be given in the examination. Choose one and write between 450 and 600 words.

Write a story based on one of the following:

A person who was injured but kept it a secret and caused her friends great trouble

The new bus driver

Write a story with the title: An Unexpected Visitor

Write a story beginning: 'I could tell by his face that he was angry'

Write a story about the rivalry between two elderly people

Chapter **9**

Directed Writing

Part Two of Paper 1 of the CIE examination contains a Directed Writing task (sometimes referred to as Transactional Writing). This differs from the continuous writing tasks contained in Part 1 as some marks are awarded for evidence that you have read the information given in the question carefully as well as for your writing skills. As with all writing tasks it tests those Assessment Objectives concerned with organisation of paragraphs, correct use of vocabulary, grammar, punctuation, spelling and the use of Standard English. In particular, however, it focuses on the following aspects of the Assessment Objectives:

ii. use language to inform and explain

iii. show an awareness of how written communication varies according to situation, purpose and audience

v. select, retrieve, evaluate and combine information from written texts

vii. employ different forms of writing to suit a range of purposes

Here is an example of a typical Directed Writing task:

Your local youth group has arranged a camping trip for its members. As Secretary of the group, you have to write a letter to the parents of all those wishing to go on the trip informing them of the arrangements involved. As some parents may be concerned about the safety of their sons/daughters, you should, in your letter, attempt to reassure them of the precautions which are in place.

Include in your letter the following information:

* When and where the trip will take place
* Travel arrangements to and from the camp site
* Cost of the trip
* Activities involved
* Safety precautions

Begin your letter, 'Dear Parent...'

Exercise 1

Now let us consider more closely what this task involves:

- You have been given a **situation** (the camping trip), a **character** or **persona** in which to write (secretary of a youth group), an **audience** to address (parents) and a **genre** (a letter).

- You have been given 5 specific points of detail to include in your letter.

- It is important that the letter you write is **fit for purpose**.

- The **tone** and **register** you use are, therefore, particularly important.

- Your approach should be friendly but not too informal. You should try both to encourage parents to let their children take part in the trip and also to reassure them of the safety aspects involved.

- The information concerning details of the trip should be given clearly and unambiguously.

- You have been told how to begin the letter; there is no need to put your address at the top although you may want to make up a contact telephone number to include in the letter at an appropriate point.

- You should plan the order of your paragraphs carefully to ensure that all points are clearly communicated in a logical and reader-friendly way.

- Of the five points which must be included some, such as the cost and dates of the trip, simply need to be stated clearly; however, details of the activities involved and the safety precautions will need some suitable elaboration.

- The opening and concluding paragraphs are particularly important in establishing an appropriate tone for your letter.

- Remember that your letter requires a suitable **valediction** (Yours sincerely) and you should include your position (Secretary) after your signature.

Now, plan and write your letter, using the notes above.

Forms and Purposes

Assessment Objective (vii) states that you are required to employ different forms of writing to suit a range of purposes. This is most directly tested in the Directed Writing tasks. Although only one task is set in each examination paper, over a period of years, different forms of writing and different purposes for writing will be tested. It is important that you become familiar with the requirements needed for each of the main forms of writing that may occur. These are: letters; speeches/ talks; reports.

Letters

Letters may be either formal or informal. For example, you may be required to write a letter to a magazine or a newspaper; to a company or organisation asking for information or complaining about something; to a friend or acquaintance asking for their support in a venture you are undertaking or apologizing for something which happened.

Of the above examples, the letters to a newspaper or an organisation are likely to be formal and that to a relative or acquaintance will be informal.

As a general rule, if you begin your letter by addressing the person to whom you are writing by his or her position or title (e.g. Dear Editor, Dear Sir/Madam) then you are using a formal register. However, if you are addressing the person by name (e.g. Dear Mr Miah or Dear Rafiq or Dear Aunt Urmi), then you are writing informally. Different letter conventions apply, depending upon which sort of letter you are writing.

Formal letters should begin with your address and the date in the top right hand corner of the page and with the title and address of the person to whom you are writing on the left hand side of the page, starting below the last line of your address. The salutation (Dear Mr...) should be written directly under the last line of the recipient's address and, if you have been asked to quote a reference, this should be placed on the middle of the following line. Your letter should conclude with either 'Yours faithfully' or 'Yours truly' and you should sign both your first name and surname or family name. See for example p.83.

Informal or **personal** letters are, by their very nature, less detailed in their layout. Again, your address and the date should be written in the top right hand corner of the page but it is not necessary to include the recipient's address.

Your address

Date

Recipient's name and title

Recipient's address

Dear Mr...........

Ref: AXGTY/2007

_____

_____

_____

_____

_____

_____

_____

_____

_____

Yours faithfully

You should place the salutation (Dear Urmi) at the left of the page on the line immediately below the date. If you address the person by their title and name (Dear Mrs Patel) then you should conclude the letter with the standard valediction for a personal letter which is 'Yours sincerely'; however, if you are writing to a close friend or relative, 'Yours sincerely' usually sounds too stilted so you need to decide on a valediction which reflects the closeness of your relationship to the recipient such as 'With love' or 'Yours affectionately'.

A personal letter will, therefore, look something like this:

Your address

Date

Dear Urmi

_____

_____

_____

_____

_____

_____

_____

_____

_____

_____

_____

With lots of love

Soraya

The main difference between a personal and impersonal letter will be found in the tone of what you write. Formal letters will be more objective in tone and written in formal Standard English; personal letters will be more colloquial with a greater use of abbreviations. Similarly, formal letters will focus almost exclusively on the issue with which they are concerned, whereas personal letters are likely to ask questions about the recipient's health and that of his or her family as well as dealing with the main topic of the letter. However, you should be careful not to make an informal letter so colloquial that an examiner reading it cannot understand what is being said.

The advice above is concerned with the format to be used when writing letters in everyday situations; as already stated, letters set as part of Directed Writing tasks in examinations will not require you to give details of the sender's or recipient's addresses unless such details are provided for you in the instructions to the question. You should, however, always include an appropriate date.

Letter Writing Exercise

Choose **one** of the topics below and write an appropriate letter:

i. You have recently bought an expensive piece of electronic equipment which has developed a fault. Write a letter to the retailer explaining when you bought the item, what the fault is, and asking for either a full refund or a brand new replacement for the item.

ii. Write a letter to your aunt who lives in another town. You are visiting that town for the purpose of attending an interview and you wish to ask your aunt if she could provide you with overnight accommodation for two nights.

iii. Write a letter to the Editor of a local newspaper, in which you explain why there should be more leisure facilities provided for young people of your age group in your local area and asking for support from other people in your campaign for suitable facilities.

Speeches and Talks

If you are asked to write the words of either a speech or a talk, it is important that you show some awareness of an oral register in your writing. A speech is generally a more formal form of spoken address than a talk and is likely to be aimed at a larger audience. For example, a talk may be addressed to members of your own class at school, whereas, a speech could be delivered as part of a public speaking competition to an audience with whom you are unfamiliar. In the latter case, it would be sensible to begin your response by introducing yourself ('Good evening, my name is and I am going to speak about...') whereas, with the former such an introduction would be unnecessary as your listeners would already know who you are; in this case, your introduction could be much more low-key ('Hello, everyone, you all know me and you won't be surprised that I am going to talk to you about...'). Remember, also, that both speeches and talks may require you to be persuasive or informative and you should ensure that the register you use is appropriate to the task.

The instructions to the task will indicate who your audience is. It is important that you keep this audience clearly in mind while you are writing your response as you will be rewarded for the use of a tone which is appropriate to the audience. For example, if you are addressing an audience of 16-year-old students within a school classroom your language is likely to be more colloquial than if you are addressing an audience of local dignitaries, teachers and parents at a school speech day.

One of the main difficulties when writing the words of a speech or a talk for the purpose of answering an examination question is to ensure that what you write sounds like something which is spoken but avoids being so informal in its structure and vocabulary that it is difficult to assess as an example of Standard English. The best approach is to ensure that you place your words clearly within an oral framework by starting with a direct address to your audience and concluding in a similar way ('Thank you for listening to what I have had to say.'). Once you have given yourself this type of structure then try to ensure that, at regular points throughout your speech, you address your audience directly (through the use of the either the second person pronoun *you* or the inclusive first person plural *we*) and that you include your audience in what you are saying by directing rhetorical questions towards them. Much as the speech genre is a central element of the question, you should not concentrate on this at the expense of the structure of your argument and the need to include the points stated in the question.

Finally, it is not necessary to embellish what you write with stage directions such as '(Spoken passionately, while raising both arms in the air)'; as a successful writer will convey emotions and so on through well-chosen vocabulary and a suitable variety of sentence structures.

Speech/talk writing exercise

You have been asked to talk to a small group of students in your year group at school about a local tradition or ceremony which you consider to be important. In your talk you should:

- explain what the tradition or ceremony is
- when and where it is practised
- what it involves
- why it is so important to you and your family and friends
- why it should be preserved.

Reports

There are two possible types of report that you may be required to write as a Directed Writing exercise. One is a report for a newspaper or magazine giving an account of an event or an episode; the other is a formal report written to be read by someone in authority (the Principal of a school or the police) in which you provide information about something which you have witnessed or in which you have assembled facts and details to support a particular proposition (such as suggestions for redesigning a student common room).

Whichever type of report you write, it is important that you organise your response carefully as you must ensure that the facts you are communicating are followed easily by the reader. You should keep the audience for your report in mind at all times and write using a register appropriate to that person's position. Remember that, with a formal report, the person for whom you are writing is likely to be busy and will not, therefore, appreciate something that is too full of digressions and unnecessary description and does not convey the facts directly.

As a general rule, you should include a main heading at the start of your report ('Proposals for Redesigning the Students' Common Room'). Each paragraph should contain one key point and the topic sentence should clearly state what this is and point the way forward. At the end of the report there should be a business-like summing up of the main points with a suggestion as to the next stages to be considered if the task requires this.

If you are asked to write a report for a newspaper or magazine then certain specific features need to be considered. One of these is that it may be necessary to make the report more immediate or dramatic than would be the case with a formal report. Newspaper reports, in particular, should start with a headline which will prepare the reader for both the facts and the tone of what follows. They may also contain statements given by other people who were present at the incident being reported. These statements can be written either as reported speech or included in your report as direct quotations (in which case it is, of course, important that you punctuate them correctly as direct speech).

Report writing exercise

An incident occurred in your English lesson the other day. Your teacher had had to leave the room on urgent business and while s/he was gone, a window was accidentally broken. As the class representative, the Principal has asked you for a formal written report to explain what happened. Your report should include the following details:

- why the teacher had to leave the room
- whether anybody had been left in charge
- what happened
- who was involved
- was anyone at fault

Examples of Directed Writing responses

Here are examples of the responses of two examination candidates to the same task. Read each through carefully and discuss its strengths and weaknesses with a partner. In particular, make notes on how well the writers have dealt with the following features:

- Layout
- Tone
- Treatment of required details
- Arrangement of ideas
- Suitability of salutation and valediction

Task

You have been chosen to represent your school in a general knowledge competition. You must choose one friend to be in your team.

Write a letter to your friend inviting him or her to be in your team. You must include the following points:

- When and where the competition will take place
- A request to your friend to join you in the team
- Why you think your friend is the best choice for your team
- What preparation you should both do
- Details of the prizes in the competition

You must cover all five points in detail. You may also add further details if you wish. Make your letter friendly and enthusiastic. Start with 'Dear…'.

Answer 1

Dear Sanjeev

It has been a very long time since I ever spent with you or even seen you. This is why I am writing to you, to inform you that there is a general knowledge competition that I believe that you and I could win together. I am writing you to become part of our team and take yet another tittle.

The competition will be held in my school hall, where you and I captured our first ever public speaking tittle. The competition will be held on 16 November 2007 which gives us a month to prepare for the competition.

In general preparation, our General Studies teacher, Mrs Charles, has prepared some notes to further our general knowledge. This will help us tremendously and reduce the time taken to research information. I think that this information will be retained in your mind easily for you understand work easily.

I advise that you enter the competition for the prizes is worth the work and time. The third prize is fifty thousand rupees to be shared amongst the team. The second is sixty thousand rupees and three computer towards our school. The first prize is seventy five thousand rupees also to be shared and five computers towards the school.

I strongly believe that you are the best person to join our team and fill the vacant space. Your mental capacity and quick understanding can help our team to be victorious. Please reply as soon as possible to inform me of your choice.

Yours truly
Sunil

Answer 2

Dear Yash

How's life with you? I hope everything is fine. Please give my regards to the rest of your family. As I have already told you, I have been named captain of the team which will represent our school in the forthcoming general knowledge competition organised by the Rotary Club. The competition will take place on the 25 November during the summer holidays so it does not clash with our end-of-year examinations. The Rotary Club has already reserved the Town Hall for the occasion.

The team consists of three members and I would be glad if you would be one of them. I have already asked Leena and she agrees with me that I should invite you to join us. I sincerely hope that you will as I'm looking forward to working with you.

I believe you are the best choice for our team because I know you travel abroad quite frequently. I'm sure your vast experience of foreign countries will be an important catalyst in our success. I also chose you as you have been learning Biology, a subject which neither Leena nor I has studied.

If you agree to form part of our team, please make a list and learn everything you can about important towns and cities abroad like London, Paris, New York etc. Leena is studying as much history as she can of all the places she can think of. I have taken up researching details of celebrities and major sporting achievements. I know our teamwork will be central to our success.

The winners of the competition will each receive a cheque for 5000 rupees and a week long holiday to a top hotel in Mauritius with all expenses paid. I will be thrilled if you accept this request. Please reply as soon as possible; I must stop now or I'll miss the post.

Best regards
Sarwan

Both of these responses cover all the required points for inclusion but the second is a more successful response for various reasons. It is better organised; it has a more consistently persuasive tone and it develops details relating, in particular, to the preparation for the task in more convincing detail. Whereas, the first answer contains an inappropriate valediction ('Yours truly'), the second uses exactly the right formula for a letter to a friend ('Best regards'). It should also be noted that the written expression of Answer 1 is less accurate than that of Answer 2.

Finally, here is a selection of Descriptive Writing tasks similar to those that you will be given in the examination. Choose one and write between 200 and 300 words.

i.   There have been some unusual noises every night of the last five nights near where you live. They happened at the same time and in the same way each night. Your family and neighbours are very upset. Last night you saw what happened and you now decide to report to the police.

Write your report. You **must** include the following information:

* at what time **and** where this occurred
* what exactly happened
* who was involved
* why your family and the neighbours are so upset
* what you want the police to do

You must cover all five points in detail. You could also add further details if you wish and make your report clear and helpful.

ii. You have just heard that a relative of yours is in hospital for a minor operation. You have decided to write a letter intended to express your concern. You should:

* say how sorry you are
* ask about the patient's well-being
* give some light-hearted news from home
* suggest a home-coming party
* promise a visit

Using all five points above, write the letter to your relative. You may add details of your own if you wish.

Make sure that your English is correct and the letter is cheerful.

iii. Your school is holding a writing competition. You are asked to write an article about a person with whom you would like to change places for a day. It could be a famous person or someone you know. Write your article which will appear in your school magazine. You must include the following:

- a suitable headline for your article
- which person you would like to change places with
- what you admire about that person
- what you would do on that day
- what you think you would learn from changing places with that person

You must cover all five points in detail. You should add further details if you wish and make your article lively and interesting for your fellow students.

iv. While shopping in your local market you witnessed a theft take place. Although many stallholders and customers chased, the thief was not caught. The police were called and they asked all witnesses to write a report of what they saw.

Write your report; you must include the following details:

- when and where the theft took place
- how the theft was carried out
- a description of the thief
- what other people were present and what they did
- why the thief escaped capture

You may add other details if you wish but make sure that your report is focussed on the episode.

v. You have just returned from a three-day outdoor activity camp. You have decided to write a letter to a friend about your experiences at the camp. Write your letter including the details below:

- who organised the camp
- where and when it took place
- the accommodation in which you stayed
- the activities in which you took part
- the benefits you gained from the experience

You may add further relevant details if you wish.

Paper (1) Frequently asked questions

> **Question**
> Will I be penalised if I write less than the recommended word limits?

Answer

The examiner will not apply a specific mark deduction for answers which are slightly less than the recommended number of words although such answers are likely to be self-penalising as ideas may not be developed fully. This could result in your being awarded a slightly lower mark than if your answer had been of the required length. However, if your answer is less than 150 words in length then it will be marked out of a maximum of 20 marks.

The same principle applies to the Directed Writing task in Part 2. If you write fewer than 100 words, then the maximum mark you can be awarded for Language/Style is 8.

> **Question**
> Will I be penalised if my answers are longer than the recommended word limits?

Answer

No, but it is likely that by writing too much, especially for Part 1, you will penalise yourself. When you are writing under timed, examination conditions, the more you write, the less time you will have for planning and checking your work which means that there is a greater chance of making careless mistakes of written expression which the examiner will penalise. Remember, also, that if you write too much for Part 1, you will leave yourself insufficient time to produce an adequate answer for Part 2.

> **Question**
> Will I lose marks for every spelling and punctuation mistake I make?

Answer

No. Your writing will be assessed by overall impression in which the examiner takes into account the linguistic competence you display as well as the relevance and interest of what you write; the more easily you communicate your meaning to the examiner, the higher the mark you will be given. However, if your answer contains so many errors of expression, punctuation and spelling that the examiner's understanding of what you want to say is impeded and she or he has to re-read what you have written to make sense out of it, then you will be given a mark in one of the lower bands.

Question

If I write a really interesting and exciting story, will this compensate for making spelling and grammatical mistakes?

Answer

Only to some extent. The main purpose of the writing task is to assess your linguistic competence; if your expression is not secure, then you will not be fully successful in conveying an exciting piece of work. Remember that you can make what you write interesting by successful vocabulary choices and controlled, positive punctuation. Do not try to write something which is too ambitious; you will run into time difficulties.

Question

If I'm not sure how to spell a word, but think it is the best one to use, should I use it anyway?

Answer

Yes. Examiners are always prepared to reward good, precise use of vocabulary so, as long as the word can be recognised, it is likely that the positive merit of the vocabulary choice will compensate for the fact that there may be a slip in the spelling. The spelling errors which are most serious are those where you misspell simple vocabulary (e.g. freind, dinning room) or when you misspell the same word in different ways in different parts of your essay.

Question

How are the marks allocated for the Directed Writing task in Part 2?

Answer

A maximum of 15 marks is available for the linguistic expression and style of your answer; a further 5 marks are available for including the content points required by the question. Overall, the linguistic qualities the examiner will be looking for are very similar to those required for the essay in Part 1. However, there will be a particular emphasis placed on how well your answer suits the purpose of the task. For example, if you are required to write a friendly letter, it is important that you write in an appropriate tone and are not overly formal; if you are asked to write a newspaper report then you should show an awareness of the common features of journalistic style etc.

Question

How much detail should I give to making the content points?

Answer

It is not enough to just mention the points. The examiner will want to see that you have fully understood the point and this means that you should develop each point sufficiently to show that it has been made clearly. When you are planning your answer for Part 2 it is a good idea to use the content points as the basis of your plan so that you can give a clear focus to each point and make it an essential part of your answer. Remember to be precise; if you are asked to give the date when an event occurred, do not just write something general like 'last week' as this is unlikely to provide sufficiently detailed information; the actual day and date would be much more useful.

Question

Is it possible to gain full marks for an answer to a writing task?

Answer

Yes, as long as your answer fulfils all the requirements of the top band in the examiner's mark scheme. Although full mark responses are not common, examiners will award top marks for a piece of writing which is consistently of an excellent quality. The occasional slip will not prevent full marks being awarded as examiners are fully aware of the difficulties of writing under examination conditions.

Paper (1) **Practice Examination**

Finally, here is a complete 'O' Level Paper 1 for you to answer. Try to complete it in the time allowed and make sure that you put into practice all the advice you have picked up from previous chapters.

Part One

Write on one of the following topics. At the head of your composition put the number of the topic you have chosen.

You are advised to spend about 60 minutes on this part of the paper and to write between 300 and 600 words.

Total marks for this part: 40

1. Describe someone you know personally who is a mixture of attractive qualities and odd behaviour.

2. If you could live for a month in any other country, which would it be and why?

3. Write about an occasion when someone reacted too quickly and spoilt a perfectly, sensible scheme. (N.B. You must not repeat a story you have encountered elsewhere.)

4. Imagine you have started a job. Write about a perfect day or a disastrous one.

5. Write a story based on the sentence: "Only when we rushed into the library did we understand why he had shouted out." (N.B. You must not repeat a story you have encountered elsewhere.)

Part Two

Begin your answer on a fresh page. You are advised to spend about 30 minutes on this part of the paper and to write between 200 and 300 words.

Total marks for this part: 20

You have recently been the victim of a minor crime in a public place. When you read the account of the incident in the local newspaper you are angry to discover that the reporter thinks you are the guilty person. You decide to write a letter to the Editor to convince him of the truth.

Write your letter to the Editor. You **must** include the following information:

- when and where the incident took place
- who else was involved
- what the report said had happened
- what really happened
- a request for an apology to be published in the newspaper

You must cover all five points **in detail**. You should also add further details if you wish and adopt a suitable tone.

Chapter **10**

Introduction to Paper 2

Paper 2 in 'O' Level English Language is the Comprehension Paper. It lasts for 1 hour and 30 minutes and in total is worth 50 marks. You will be given a passage to read, of around 1250 to 1350 words. The passage may be fiction narrative or non-fiction discursive.

The first 25 marks are allocated to answering a number of comprehension questions of differing types. These types of questions are likely to be a combination of literal, or fact gathering, comprehension questions, inferential comprehension questions, questions on the writer's craft, vocabulary questions, quotation questions, two part questions and questions where you are required to answer in your own words. Do not worry if at this stage this list is very daunting: one of the purposes of this textbook is to take you through the various types of possible questions so that you are able to recognise them and then answer them skilfully.

The second 25 marks are allocated to writing a summary of a section of the passage, around 750 words of the original. You will be asked to reduce the original 750 words or so to 160 words of your own. You will be required to pick out as many content points as you can from a selection of around twenty, for each of which you will be given one mark to a maximum of fifteen marks. You will be asked to write your summary in formal, continuous prose. You will be given ten introductory words to ease you into the summary and to make a good start which will give you confidence. As with the other types of questions in Paper 2, you will be given plenty of help in this textbook in breaking down the various stages in the production of a good piece of summary writing.

In order to do well in Paper 2, you will need to achieve the following Assessment Objectives:

  ii. use language to inform and explain

  iii. show an awareness of how spoken and written communication varies according to situation, purpose and audience

  iv. read a variety of texts accurately and with confidence

v. select, retrieve, evaluate and combine information from written texts

vi. appreciate the ways writers make use of language

viii. plan, organise and paragraph, using appropriate punctuation

ix. choose a vocabulary which is suited to its purpose and audience, and use correct grammar and punctuation

x. write in Standard English

xi. spell accurately the words within the working vocabulary

xii. write legibly and present finished work clearly and attractively.

You will be tested in these Assessment Objectives in different ways and through different types of questions in Paper 2. Keep in mind the directions about time constraint which are outlined in the section of this book on Paper 1. You are working against the clock in Paper 2 as well as on Paper 1, and so some sort of time management is necessary. It is pointless to spend five minutes agonising over a one mark question with which you are finding difficulty; it is much better to press on to the summary, which carries half the marks on the paper. On the other hand, it is a mistake to think that time spent reading is time wasted; it is crucial to read the passage twice before beginning to answer the questions, and you should read the area for summary again at least once when you get to the summary question so that you understand not only the passage, but how it has to be used in the context of the rubric, that is the task you are given in the summary question. It is important to strike a balance between reading and writing in Paper 2, and the best way to arrive at this balance is to practice. The aim of this section of the book is to give you that necessary practice in manageable and progressive sections.

Chapter **11**

Reading a variety of texts

In the Introduction to this section of the book, we looked at the Assessment Objectives, which are the criteria used by examiners to judge the candidates for the examination that you will eventually sit. The extent to which you demonstrate understanding of, and skill in, these Assessment Objectives will determine how well you will do in your 'O' Level examination in Paper 2.

Assessment Objective iv tests candidates' ability 'to read a variety of texts accurately and with confidence'. Almost certainly you are already doing that, even if you have never stopped to think about it.

Exercise 1

Working with a partner, make a list of the different types of written English to be found in your own homes.

The most obvious types will be books, and the most obvious division of books is into non-fiction and fiction.

Exercise 2

Working with a partner, divide your list of types of written English into non-fiction and fiction.

For non-fiction, you might have something like this: biography, autobiography, travel, information books on, for example, sport or entertainment. But other non-fiction material in your home might also include recipe books, a telephone directory, magazines, and manuals on, for example, a computer or a washing machine.

For fiction texts, you might have something like this: science fiction, war, historical, crime, romance, human interest, thriller, adventure, school, childhood. These broad headings for fiction texts are called **genres**.

In Paper two of your examination, your ability to read 'a variety of texts' is tested. The more experience you have of reading written English on your own will clearly be linked to your ability to succeed in an examination. The passage on which you are tested in the examination will be fiction or non-fiction. If it is fiction, it may come from any genre, and if it is non-fiction it may be from any one of a variety of topics, whether about modern issues or topics of a more historical nature. One way to prepare for the examination, therefore, is to familiarise yourself with different types of written English and be able to recognise the characteristics of different types of written English.

Exercise 3

Working with a partner, read the following very short texts of written English. Write each one down and beside each write whether it is fiction or non-fiction.

i. The damage being done to coral reefs in the twenty-first century is a cause of great concern to governments and environmentalists alike.

ii. Standing in the shadows of the huge house's garden, he watched and waited. His opportunity would arise soon, he was sure of that.

iii. There can be no doubt that computers have brought about a revolution in the way schools are run.

iv. 'What do you want?' came the robotic voice from the other space ship. Ajay stepped forward, terrified.

v. It was a terrifying sight all right. But at least, thought Sachin, they would soon know the truth. It had been a long hard battle.

vi. It was good that the two families were pleased at the match. Already preparations were underway for the big day.

vii. The girls crowded into the assembly hall, where the results would be announced. It was hard not to be anxious, although some girls disguised it well by giggling nervously.

viii. The cinema is undoubtedly a useful and pleasant means of relaxation. It can also be educational.

ix. The men marched on, their eyes dimmed with fatigue, their feet blistered in their ill-fitting boots, the scream of dropping shells behind them.

x. Many foods contain high amounts of unsaturated fat, which is unfortunately contributing to increased levels of obesity in some parts of the world.

Exercise 4

Working with a partner, look back at the texts in the previous exercise which you have judged to be fiction. Against each, write down what genre of fiction you consider it to be. At the end of your list of texts from the previous exercise, write a sentence of your own in which, by referring closely to the language of the text, you justify your choice of genre.

Exercise 5

Write ten short texts of your own, each one not more than thirty words. Write five fiction and five non-fiction texts. It should be clear from the language of each text whether it is fiction or non-fiction, and what genre each of the five fiction texts is.

Exercise 6

Swap your ten texts with a partner. Copy each of your partner's ten texts. Beside each one write whether it is fiction or non-fiction, and, in addition, write beside each fiction text what genre it is. When both you and your partner have finished this exercise, swap your work back and correct it for each other. Take time out to explain errors which have occurred in identifying the texts.

Exercise 7

This is an exercise which must be started at home. Bring to class six types of writing from your own home. These should be a mixture of fiction and non-fiction, and different fiction genres. Prepare a short talk to the class in which you identify your texts as fiction or non-fiction, identify fiction genres, and single out features of language, e.g. particular words and phrases, which back up your identification.

The purposes of the exercises covered so far in this chapter are to highlight the different types of written English which you already know and to help you to focus on means of identifying these different types of written English. This in turn will help you to cope with whatever type of comprehension text you are asked to deal with in an examination and to sharpen your focus and hence your ability to perform well. The most basic task for you in any reading situation, whether in examinations or during your normal daily life, is to glean information, which might be no more than simple facts.

Exercise 8 Witches and Ogres

Read the following short passage, which is childhood fiction genre, and write down three pieces of information which are contained in it.

I was finding it hard going, pushing on the pedals. The tyres slipped on the stones and the clods of dry earth. The closer I got to the house, the bigger the yellow house grew in front of me, and the heavier the weight that crushed my chest, taking my breath away.

What if I arrived and found witches or an ogre there?

I knew witches met at night in abandoned houses and had parties and if you joined in you went mad and that ogres ate children.

Exercise 9 Computers in Education

Read the following short discursive passage and write down three pieces of information which are contained in it.

Computers in the classroom have brought about a revolution in education. No longer are all lessons taught by the teacher using the board and a piece of chalk, or by children reading books. These methods of learning have their place of course, and an invaluable one at that, but computers allow individual learning-children can also work at their own pace, which increases their motivation.

Exercise 10 Another Working Day

Read the following short passage, which is crime fiction genre, and write down three pieces of information which are contained in it.

Sergeant Smith was not very fond of his boss, the Chief Superintendent. But they had a reasonable working relationship, which was just as well, thought Sergeant Smith, as the two of them drove to their latest crime scene – a house where the owner had been attacked by two young men who had broken in to steal anything of value they could find, especially jewellery.

Exercise 11 The Retreat

Read the following short passage, which is war fiction genre, and write down three pieces of information which are contained in it.

The air was grey with diesel fumes, and straggling wearily through the stench, and for the moment moving faster than the traffic, were hundreds of soldiers, most of them carrying their rifles and their awkward greatcoats — a burden in the morning's growing warmth. Walking with the soldiers were families hauling suitcases, bundles, babies, or holding the hands of children. The only human sound Turner heard, piercing the din of engines, was the crying of babies.

Source: *Atonement* by Ian McEwan, Vintage

Exercise 12   Space Travel

Read the following short discursive passage and write down three pieces of information which are contained in it.

Perhaps the strongest proof of the ingenuity of mankind is the fact that human beings have begun the exploration of space. People in the second half of the twentieth century saw men walking on the surface of the moon, which a short time before must have seemed more like science fiction than reality. Spacecraft in orbit has become a familiar, if not a commonplace, phenomenon, and we are no longer surprised to hear about the exploration of space in newspapers or television.

Exercise 13   Nelson Mandela

Read the following short passage of autobiography and write down three pieces of information which are contained in it.

When I was not much more than a newborn child, my father was involved in a dispute that deprived him of his chieftainship at Mvezo and revealed a strain in his character I believe he passed on to his son. I maintain that nurture, rather than nature, is the primary moulder of personality, but my father possessed a proud sense of rebelliousness, a stubborn sense of fairness, that I recognise in myself.

Source: *Long Walk to Freedom* by Nelson Mandela, Little, Brown Book Group

Exercise 14   Examinations

Read the following short discursive passage and write down three pieces of information which are contained in it.

There can be no doubt that the examination season is a tense time for students. Months, and sometimes years, of preparation have gone into each examination, and students feel under great pressure to perform to the best of their ability and achieve their potential. Sometimes their parents, however unwittingly, add to their pressure by talking about the examination results of other members of the family, stressing how important it is to succeed at school if one is to succeed in life. Teachers, too, in their desire to prepare their classes well for the impending examinations, put an additional burden on to the poor students, who sometimes dread the possibility of letting down their hard-working teachers who have done so much for them.

Chapter **12**

More exercises in fact gathering from short texts

Exercise 1 Joseph

Read the following short passage, which is fiction school genre, and answer the fact gathering questions which follow.

Rohit always dreaded going into the chemistry class because Joseph intimidated him. No matter how hard Rohit tried, his marks for class tests just never matched up to Joseph's. Only last week, Rohit had spent hours on a detailed assignment given to the class by their teacher. At home, Rohit's finished assignment had looked splendid, but when Joseph took his own assignment out of his bag and handed it to the teacher, Rohit was dazzled by the brightness of its colourful front cover and depressed by its obvious length. The trouble was, it was difficult not to like Joseph. It would have been much simpler to dismiss him as the class swot, or some strange workaholic, but, no, Joseph was great company, with a quirky sense of humour, who looked out for everyone and was very thoughtful and kind-hearted. It wasn't his fault he was so clever.

i. Why did Rohit dread going into the chemistry class? [1]

ii. Was Rohit pleased or disappointed with his assignment as soon as he had finished it at home? [1]

iii. Did Rohit like or dislike Joseph? [1]

iv. Write down one thing about Joseph which made him a popular pupil. [1]

v. Write down the one thing about Joseph which made people wary of Joseph. [1]

[*Total: 5 marks*]

Exercise 2 Stamford Raffles

Read the following short non-fiction passage and answer the fact gathering questions which follow.

Stamford Raffles was born in 1781 on board the ship of his father, a sea-captain trading between Jamaica and London. His father was not a good businessman, and he became so poor and heavily in debt that Stamford had to leave school at the age of fourteen to work as a clerk in the London office of the East India company. They were hard times for a boy growing into a man. The office hours were long and the work dull, but the youth seized every spare minute to educate himself, reading as many books as he could, teaching himself French, and studying animals and plants. He was the only breadwinner in the family and sometimes he could not afford even a candle for his night reading. So, when, in 1805, Raffles was offered a well-paid job in Penang, he accepted it gladly.

i.	What was the occupation of Stamford Raffles' father?	[1]
ii.	Why did Stamford have to leave school at the age of fourteen?	[1]
iii.	What was Stamford's first job?	[1]
iv.	How can we tell that Stamford did not have much time for study?	[1]
v.	How can we tell that Stamford was very poor?	[1]
vi.	Why was Stamford glad to accept the job in Penang?	[1]

[*Total: 6 marks*]

Exercise 3 Maids and their Employers

Read the following short non-fiction passage and answer the fact gathering questions which follow.

The problems faced by both maids and their employers often appear in letters and articles in the media or are highlighted on television programmes. On the one hand, there are stories of laziness, arguments over what maids will do or will not do, (or can and cannot do), complaints about their attitudes to their employers and dissatisfaction with their behaviour on and off duty. On the other hand, there are accounts of inadequate time off, low wages, poor living conditions, payments in arrears, insufficient home leave and, in the worst cases, real cruelty and exploitation. It has to be said that the employers' complaints are more frequently heard, though this does not necessarily mean that they are more often in the right.

> i. Apart from letters and articles in the media, where are problems faced by maids and their employers highlighted? [1]
>
> ii. Write down one complaint that employers make about their maids. [1]
>
> iii. Write down the two most serious complaints that maids make about their employers. [1]
>
> iv. Which group, employers or maids, complains more often? [1]
>
> [*Total: 4 marks*]

Exercise 4 Anna

Read the following short passage, which is fiction childhood genre, and answer the fact gathering questions which follow.

The bus was already crowded when it arrived, and Anna and her mother barely managed to find room to sit. Off it went, rattling along over the dirt road, until it eventually trundled to a stop outside the market area. Anna's mother bundled her off, eager to join the jostling crowds thronging the narrow streets. They hurried by the displays of flashy jewellery spread out on the walk-ways, with their coloured bangles, crudely fashioned rings, and roughly polished stones, making for the stall selling clothing material. Anna's mother quickly began sifting through their repetitive patterns of colour, fashioning in her mind's eye some new dress for herself, no doubt, or a best shirt for father. Anna, however, had her mind set on the caves near the market. She had heard of the attractions there; the tempting iced drinks, street musicians performing, and the fascinating puppet shows. Up till now she had not been allowed to go on her own. For the moment, though, the displays of luscious fruit across the road were temptation enough. She counted the coins in her purse, and treated herself to a small bag of juicy plums.

> i. Why did Anna and her mother find it difficult to find a seat on the bus? [1]
>
> ii. Where were Anna and her mother going? [1]
>
> iii. Which stall were they heading for? [1]
>
> iv. What was Anna's mother thinking of making? [1]
>
> v. Where did Anna really want to go? [1]
>
> vi. Was Anna allowed to leave her mother at the market? [1]
>
> [*Total: 6 marks*]

Exercise 5 Modern Travel

Read the following short non-fiction passage and answer the fact gathering questions which follow.

In the twenty-first century, ordinary people can travel more than they were ever able to do before. One reason for this is the vast improvement in transport and communications. Jet planes can travel from one end of the world to the other in a matter of hours. People work shorter working weeks than in the past and therefore have more leisure time, which they often spend taking holidays to far-flung destinations. Places they would only ever have dreamed of, or have seen in magazines or read about in books, have become accessible to the ordinary traveller. Low price airlines are a modern phenomenon; sometimes called 'no frills' airlines, they keep prices down by cutting back on many of the extra services of their more expensive counterparts – for example, a seating plan on the plane, or elaborate meals and drinks. Affluence and higher incomes also mean that ordinary people are able to do more than feed, house, clothe and educate their families – they are able to indulge themselves in luxuries which in the past were reserved for the rich. One of the most appreciated of these luxuries is travel.

i.   In what one way, according to the writer, is the twenty-first century different from those which went before? [1]

ii. Why do people nowadays have more leisure time than in the past? [1]

iii. What is different about the destinations of the modern traveller compared to the destinations of travellers in the past? [1]

iv. How do 'no frills' airlines keep their prices down? [1]

v.   Why are ordinary people nowadays able to have luxuries which were not available to ordinary people in the past? [1]

vi. What, according to the writer, is one of the most appreciated luxuries available to ordinary people nowadays? [1]

[*Total: 6 marks*]

Exercise 6 Gerry

Read the following short passage, which is fiction school genre, and answer the questions which follow.

The day had started off badly for Gerry. Firstly, his alarm clock had not rung because, he realised later, the battery needed to be replaced. When he got up, late of course, he remembered that he had forgotten to pack his schoolbag the night before. How often his mother had told him to be well prepared for school by having an organised bag sitting at the front door. He scrambled around frantically, picking up notebooks, textbook and pencils and dashed out for the school bus. As he reached the bus stop, he was just in time to see the school bus drive off in a cloud of exhaust fumes. Feeling very sorry for himself, and feeling hunger pangs because he had not had time for breakfast, he felt like crying, although tears were, he thought, hardly appropriate for a boy of his age.

i.	Why did Gerry not wake in time for school?	[1]
ii.	What advice had Gerry's mother often given him?	[1]
iii.	How did Gerry normally get to school?	[1]
iv.	What went wrong with his travel arrangements on this particular day?	[1]
v.	Apart from feeling sorry for himself, why does Gerry feel like crying?	[1]
vi.	Why does he think he should stop himself from crying?	[1]

[Total: 6 marks]

Exercise 7 The Intruder

Read the following short passage, which is fiction crime fiction genre, and answer the fact gathering questions which follow.

He stood in the dark, at the edge of the quiet street, ready to walk quickly away if anyone passed by who might later be able to identify him. He was dressed in a nondescript way – black jogging trousers, baggy black sweater – and he had been careful to shield his eyes with a baseball cap. He would be difficult to identify, all right, although the chances of that ever becoming an issue were slim in this deserted part of town. He pulled himself back further into the shadows as the front door of the house – the house he had been watching for weeks – opened and the owner, a dark haired, rather burly man of about forty, he'd reckoned, came out and got into his parked car. As the car drove away, he smiled to himself. This was his moment. The rest of the inhabitants of the house – i.e. the mother and the two children whom she took out every Tuesday – had already left. That meant that the house was empty. It was up to him now to avail himself of this opportunity, and make his move. Having checked that no – one was around, he walked briskly in the front gate and round to the back garden, where his bag of tools – including a crowbar – had already been hidden. He grinned to himself, pleased that his weeks of planning and surveillance were about to be rewarded. 'How smart I am!' he smiled to himself, as he removed the crowbar from the bag.

i. What is the character in the story planning to do? [1]

ii. Why would he walk quickly away if anyone passed by? [1]

iii. Write down one of the things he did to make sure he would be difficult to identify. [1]

iv. Why was the matter of identification not likely to become an issue? [1]

v. How many people lived in the house? [1]

vi. Who left the house first? [1]

vii. On what day of the week does the story take place? [1]

viii. What had he already hidden in the garden? [1]

[*Total: 8 marks*]

Chapter **13**

Selecting and retrieving information

You learned earlier that Assessment Objective (v) in 'O' Level English Language is: to select, retrieve, evaluate and combine information from written texts. Now that you have examined a variety of written texts and completed some exercises on them, it is time to think about some of these key words in Assessment Objective (v) selection and retrieval of information.

How to Select and Retrieve Information

When a comprehension question in an English examination asks you to select information, you are being asked to find an answer in a text. This may seem obvious, but there are nevertheless techniques which you can learn to make this process easier and more likely to gain you marks. For example, you need to ask yourself:

- is the answer lying on the surface of the text? *or*
- is there something I need to work out?
- how long should my answer be?
- how short is my answer allowed to be?
- am I allowed to use the words of the original text?
- do I need to use my own words?
- is the question asking only about the story or argument of the text?
- is the question asking about particular features of language, e.g. figures of speech?

Literal and Inferential Comprehension

We will start with answers to the first two questions above:

- is the answer lying on the surface of the text? *or*
- is there something I need to work out?

In literal comprehension questions, the answer lies on the surface of the text. In inferential comprehension questions, you require to work something out, to make a deduction, based on the information in the text.

Example

The sky was grey and full of heavy clouds. Rain ran in little rivers down the roads and traffic was travelling much more slowly than usual.

> **Question 1**: What was the weather like that day?
>
> **Answer**: It was raining.

The answer to this question lies on the surface of the text. The word 'rain' occurs in the text and is reinforced by the reference to the cloudy sky. This is a literal comprehension question.

> **Question 2** : From the evidence given in the text, why do you think the traffic was travelling more slowly than usual?
>
> **Answer 1**: The traffic was travelling more slowly than usual because it was raining and there might have been an accident if they had travelled at a normal speed.
>
> **Answer 2**: The traffic was travelling more slowly than usual because the drivers were worried that they might skid on the wet road.
>
> **Answer 3**: The traffic was travelling more slowly than usual because there was a traffic jam.

Answers 1 and 2 are correct and would score the mark in the examination. Each answer makes a deduction, or inference, about the text, namely that, if the rain was running in little rivers down the road, it might be dangerous for drivers to proceed at their normal pace. Answer 3 is incorrect because, although it makes a deduction, that deduction is not based on the information given in the text. Answer 3 comes from the student's imagination, not the text. There is no evidence whatsoever in the text of a traffic jam.

So you have learned that the answers to literal comprehension questions lie on the surface of the text. The answers to inferential questions do not lie on the surface of the text, but can be worked out or deduced by looking at the context of the question, that is, the area of text on which the question is based. The first step in selecting the correct answer to a comprehension question is to identify whether it is literal or inferential comprehension.

Signposts towards inferential comprehension questions include:

- Why do you think...?
- Suggest a reason...
- Why might...?
- What possible explanation is there for...?
- In what way could it be thought that...?
- How can you tell that...?

Exercise 1 Literal and Inferential Questions

Write down each of the following questions. Although they are not attached to any text, it should be possible for you to tell which can be answered by literal comprehension and which require an inference to be made. Beside each one write down whether it is signposted as a literal or as an inferential question.

i. How many people were in the restaurant?

ii. What was the name of Anna's brother?

iii. Suggest a reason why the shop was empty.

iv. At what time of day is the story set?

v. What possible explanation is there for Michael's absence on that day?

vi. Why might you be surprised to find that the trip was well organised?

vii. Why did he not know where the sound was coming from?

viii. Why do you think the writer tells us that the countryside was beautiful?

ix. What colour was the girl's dress?

x. How might you be able to tell that the journey was made during the night?

Exercise 2 City Life

What follows is a short passage with questions which can be answered by literal comprehension. Read the passage carefully and then answer the questions which follow.

Many of today's major social problems have arisen because the population has been crowded into urban areas. The drawbacks of city life are obvious:

traffic, cost of living and increased crime. The advantages of city life include access to work, services, education, entertainment and friends. If the population of a city were reduced by even ten per cent, the result would be a major difference in property values and a deterioration in services paid for by public money, like transport.

i.   Give one advantage and one disadvantage of city life.   [2]

ii. Give one result of reducing the population of a city by ten per cent.   [1]

[*Total: 3 marks*]

Exercise 3   Classroom Computers

What follows is a short passage with questions which can be answered by literal comprehension. Read the passage carefully and then answer the questions which follow.

Some people are afraid that computers used in education will lead to a deterioration in educational standards. However, anyone who has ever watched kids round a classroom computer, or witnessed computer exchanges between students in classrooms separated by oceans, knows that technology can actually improve the learning experience by making it more enjoyable. Despite a common view to the contrary, computers will not become a substitute for teachers. Indeed, computers will bring together the best work of countless teachers and students.

i.   According to 'some people', what will be the result of using computers in the classroom?   [1]

ii. According to the writer, what aspect of technology leads to an improvement in education?   [1]

iii. What is the 'common view' about computers?   [1]

iv. According to the writer, what is the advantage of using computers in the classroom?   [1]

[*Total: 4 marks*]

Exercise 4   Inferential Questions

Now answer these inferential questions on both 'City Life' and 'Classroom Computers'.

> i.   If the population of a city were reduced, why do you think there would be 'a deterioration in services'?   [1]
>
> ii. Suggest a reason why the writer refers to 'kids' in the second line of the passage and to 'students' in the third line of the passage.   [2]
>
> [*Total: 3 marks*]

Now go back to some of the other questions posed at the start of this chapter:

• how long need my answer be?

• how short is my answer allowed to be?

The answer to these questions is simple. As long as you answer the question, the length of your answer doesn't matter. You will gain no extra marks for elaborate sentences. In fact, as you will almost certainly be working against the clock, it is a good idea to keep your answer to the shortest form possible, as long as you answer the question, of course.

Look back at the answers to the inferential question: From the evidence given in the text, why do you think the traffic was travelling more slowly than usual?

There were three answers for consideration, two of which were acceptable for a mark and one of which was not. Each of the answers started: The traffic was travelling more slowly than usual because... .

However, it would not have affected the correctness or otherwise of the answers if they had simply been written as:

> It was raining and there might have been an accident if they had travelled at a normal speed.

> The drivers were worried that they might skid on the wet road.

> There was a traffic jam.

All of these sentences answer the question (although the third is wrong) in a way which does not repeat the stem of the question.

What these answers do is more than selection of information. They also retrieve the information necessary to answer the question, without wasting time in words which do not contribute to a correct answer but merely pad out a correct answer.

To retrieve information is to do more than select it. It is to home in on as small an area of the text as is sufficient to answer the given question. Retrieval of information imposes a kind of economy on your answers to questions. So remember that there is no need to copy out the stem of the question when you write an answer to it.

Exercise 5 Writing Shorter Answers

What follows are some questions and answers. Even although you are not given the original texts, write shorter answers than these given below to show that your answer has been both selected and retrieved.

> i. How can you tell that the girl is upset?

Answer: It is obvious that the girl is upset because she is crying.

> ii. If the people had realised that the storm was coming, what precaution might they have taken?

Answer: If the people had realised that the storm was coming they would have taken the precaution of tying up all the boats in the harbour.

> iii. From your reading of the passage, how many days was the journey likely to last?

Answer: From my reading of the passage it seems likely that the journey would last six days.

> iv. Suggest a reason why, in spite of the rising cost of materials, the factory continued to manufacture furniture.

Answer: In spite of the rising cost of materials, the factory continued to manufacture furniture because it had been given a subsidy by the government.

> v. The writer refers to 'an often expressed' fear. What is this fear?

Answer: The 'often expressed fear' to which the writer refers is the fear that soon there will be a shortage of teachers.

> vi. The writer states that 'technology should be at the service of everyone'. Does he fear that one group of citizens will be the only group to benefit?

Answer: He fears that, although technology should be at the service of everyone, the only group to benefit will be the rich.

vii. Feelings between the two men became strained. From the evidence of the paragraph, what is the first example of this tension?

Answer: The first example of feelings between the two men becoming strained was when they stopped talking on the journey.

viii. 'Each man looked after himself'. What is surprising about this in view of the journey they were undertaking?

Answer: It was surprising that each man looked after himself in view of the journey they were taking because it was a dangerous journey and it would have been safer if they had worked together.

ix. Apart from feelings of wild excitement, how was Emma feeling at the end of the marathon?

Answer: Apart from feelings of wild excitement, Emma was feeling exhausted at the end of the marathon.

In the following exercises, you will find passages with questions for you to answer. Use the signposts you have learned to decide which questions are literal and which are inferential. It is best to answer in sentences, but remember not to waste time in repeating the stems of the questions in your answers.

Exercise 6 Exploring a cave

Read the passage and then answer the questions which follow below.

Exploring a cave can be an unpleasant experience: there is a damp, sometimes dusty smell which seems to be the same in all caves. You can see nothing at first but, when your eyes adjust to your unfamiliar surroundings, the strange light casts eerie shadows on the walls. Sometimes you are aware of creatures like mice scurrying across you path.

If you are exploring a low cave, at the start of the walk stooping is rather a joke, but it is a joke that wears off as soon as you have travelled a short distance. You not only have to bend; you have also got to keep your head up so that you can see the roof of the cave. You have, therefore, a constant pain in the neck and aching thighs, but this is nothing compared to the pain in your knees. After about a kilometre it becomes an unbearable agony. You begin to worry whether you will ever get to the end – still more, how on earth you are going to get back. Your pace grows slower and slower in response to the difficulties. Sometimes it is hard going underneath your feet, with jagged pieces of rock littering the ground and frequent pools of stagnant water. You certainly need to tread very slowly.

i. Why does the writer describe exploring a cave as 'unpleasant'? [1]

ii. What does the writer suggest is frightening about exploring a cave? [1]

iii. What would happen to someone walking in a cave who didn't keep his head up? [2]

iv. What is the worst pain experienced by someone walking in a low cave.? [1]

v. What are the two main worries of a person walking in a low cave? [2]

vi. .Why do you think a walker's pace 'grows slower and slower'? [1]

vii. What two aspects of the cave mean that the walker 'needs to tread very slowly'? [2]

[*Total: 10 marks*]

Exercise 7   Valladolid

Read the passage and then answer the questions which follow below.

The car had dropped me in the middle of Valladolid on a hot, dusty evening. There was little life to be seen in the dim, lonely alleyways; the street lamps themselves seemed to be shrouded by a mysterious, thick light. I felt that uneasy state of mind on arriving at night in an unknown city – a faint, unsettling panic which somehow springs from the buildings all around until one has found a bed and lodgings.

But I found a house advertising lodgings. I asked the landlord for a bed for the night, and he just scowled at me without replying. Then he simply jerked his head to the door of a room nearby. Inside I found a huge, brass bed, the only piece of furniture that looked intact; everything else seemed to have been devastated by previous lodgers. Yet I felt happier. I was established; I had a room in the city of Valladolid.

I was awakened next morning by the high, clear voice of a boy singing in the street outside. As I lay there, listening, I thought that this was how it should always be: to be gently eased from sleep by a voice like this, and brought back softly to life. How different from the customary loud shouts and the knocking on the door, the alarm bells of everyday life! They came like blows on the head; they jerked you into consciousness and dragged you into wakefulness.

Source: *As I Walked One Midsummer Morning* by Laurie Lee, Penguin Books

i. Give two reasons for the writer's 'uneasy state of mind' when he Valladolid arrived in that night. [2]

ii. What was the first task the writer set himself when he arrived in Valladolid? [1]

iii. Why was the bed the only piece of furniture in the room? [1]

iv. Using the information in the whole of the second paragraph, why do you think it might be surprising that at the writer 'felt happier'. [2]

v. What woke the writer from sleep? [1]

iv. How is the writer used to being wakened? [1]

vii. Why do you think the writer describes his normal method of waking up as being 'jerked into consciousness'? [2]

[*Total: 10 marks*]

Chapter 14

More exercises in literal and inferential comprehension

Each of the exercises which follow gives you a passage to read, and for each passage there are some literal and inferential questions for you to answer. You are free to lift the answers from the passage.

Exercise 1 Julia

She had lived most of her life alone. Her mother had borne her late in life and Julia believed that the strain of trying to please her tyrannical father had probably contributed to her mother's early death. When her mother died, a few weeks after her sixtieth birthday, Julia was not quite fifteen.

She had escaped from her father as soon as she could, going to Girton College, Cambridge on a scholarship, which paid her way. Although he had tried to make her departure from the family home as unpleasant as possible, there was not much he could do to prevent it and once away from him a part of her had felt she could never again face living with another man. There had been female friends, such as Vera, and there had been Harriet whom, she now concluded, pounding the streets, she had not treated as well as she could have done. Harriet had been more than a friend; but, blindly, she had taken Harriet for granted. Yet she had loved Harriet, she now knew, and she knew it because she had learned to love someone else.

If you spend most of your life alone often you do not know that you are lonely. It was not until the 'discovery' that Julia Garnet knew that she was lonely and that she had been so for most of her life.

Source: *Miss Garnet's Angel* by Sally Vickers, Harper Collins Publishers Ltd.

> i. Give two reasons given by the writer to explain why Julia's mother died relatively young. Number your answer (a) and (b). [2]
>
> ii. How old was Julia when her mother died? [1]
>
> iii. What piece of information are we given about the behaviour of Julia's father which suggests that Julia did not have a good relationship with him? [1]

iv. Why was Julia's father unable to prevent her taking up her university place? [1]

v. Once she left home, what effect did Julia's relationship with her father have on her? [1]

vi. What two aspects of her relationship with Harriet does Julia now regret? Number your answers (a) and (b). [2]

vii. What does the word 'blindly' suggest about Julia's behaviour towards Harriet? [1]

viii. How does Julia now know that she loved Harriet? [1]

ix. According to the writer, what often happens to people who live most of their lives alone? [1]

x. Why do you think the writer begins and ends the extract with a reference to the fact that Julia has lived most of her life alone? [1]

[*Total: 12 marks*]

Exercise 2 Selling the Flat

There were matters to attend to: the solicitors, Mr Akbar. And it's right too, she thought, as the plane taxied out and up and over the sea. There is a life to close down.

London was dirty and hot after a cold July, and Ealing particularly stuffy. Mr Akbar, however, was overjoyed to see her.

'Madam, come in, come in,' he gestured hospitably down her own hall. 'It is wonderful that you have come.'

He made her sweet mint tea and they sat on the balcony overlooking the gardens. The gardens, which had been a source of joy to Julia during her years at Cedar Court, looked seedy: the turf parched and the flowerbeds municipal.

'These I love,' said Mr Akbar, pointing at a pair of bedraggled mallard ducks which had wandered onto the lawns.

'Do you, Mr Akbar? Then I am happy you are going to buy my flat.'

'You accept my price?'

Julia had taken the precaution of visiting a local estate agency before their meeting and had gleaned that the sum he was offering was rather below the market value. She had come intending to be firm on this point. But the eyes of Mr Akbar, looking pleadingly at her, made her waver. She had bought the flat for a good price after the original landlord died, leaving her as the sitting tenant. It seemed greedy to take advantage now of her own good fortune and besides, had Mr Akbar not made overtures to her she might never have had the idea to sell up. He did not have the appearance of wealth. And the hassle of selling the place elsewhere would delay her. Anyway, she owed him something for putting the idea of her permanent remove to Venice into her head.

Source: *Miss Garnet's Angel* by Sally Vickers, Harper Collins Publishers Ltd

> i. Julia plans to 'close down' her life in London. What is the first thing she has to do? [1]
>
> ii. Give three pieces of evidence to suggest that Mr Akbar 'was overjoyed to see' Julia. Number your answers (a), (b) and (c). [3]
>
> iii. Mr Akbar and Julia 'sat on the balcony'. How can you tell that Julia's feelings about her former home have changed? [1]
>
> iv. How does the writer make it clear from her description of the gardens that the weather was hot? [1]
>
> v. Why might it be surprising that Mr Akbar loves the ducks? [1]
>
> vi. What had Julia discovered when she visited the local estate agent? [1]
>
> vii. Before she came to visit Mr Akbar, what had Julia planned to do when it came to selling the house to him? [1]
>
> viii. What made Julia change her mind about her earlier decision? [1]
>
> ix. What had been Julia's 'good fortune'? [1]
>
> x. Apart from the difficulty involved in selling her flat to someone else, give two reasons why Julia decides to accept Mr Akbar's offer. Number your answers (a) and (b). [2]
>
> [*Total: 13 marks*]

Exercise 3 Easter Island

Our main difference from chimps and gorillas – with whom we share a common ancestor – is that over the past three million years or so, we have been shaped less and less by nature and more and more by culture. Therefore, we have become experimental creatures of our own making. With the discovery of agriculture, which began about 10, 000 years ago, and the consequent growth in civilisation, our experiment on material progress began to expand and accelerate; it is now moving very quickly and on a colossal scale. We have reached a stage where we must bring the experiment under rational control. If we fail – if we blow up or degrade the biosphere so it can no longer sustain us – nature will merely shrug and conclude that letting apes run the laboratory was fun for a while but in the end a bad idea.

The wrecks of our failed experiments lie in deserts and jungles like fallen airliners whose flight recorders can tell us what went wrong. Unlike written history, which is often highly edited, archaeology can uncover the deeds we have accidentally forgotten, or choose to forget.

The devastation of Easter Island is a case in point. On Easter Day, 1722, a Dutch fleet in the South Seas sighted an unknown island so treeless and eroded that they mistook its barren hills for dunes. They were amazed as they drew near to see hundreds of great stone images, some as tall as Amsterdam houses.

Captain Cook later confirmed the island's desolation, finding no wood for fuel, nor any fresh water worth taking on board. Nature, he concluded, 'had been exceedingly sparing of her favours in this spot'. The great mystery of Easter Island was that the stones seemed to have been put there without tackle, as if set down from the sky.

We now know the answer to the riddle, and it is a chilling one. Nature had not been unusually stingy with her favours. Pollen studies of the island's crater lakes have shown that it was once well-watered and green, with rich volcanic soil supporting thick woods. No natural disaster had changed that: no eruption, drought or disease. The catastrophe on Easter Island was man.

i. Give one way in which man is similar to chimps and gorillas. [1]

ii. In what main way does man differ from chimps and gorillas? [1]

iii. According to the writer, what has been the result of man having been shaped by culture? [1]

iv. What was the first result of 'the discovery of agriculture'? [1]

v. Explain fully what will happen if we do not control 'our experiment on material progress'. [2]

vi. According to the writer, in what way does written history differ from archaeology? [1]

vii. What two types of events does archaeology inform us about which written history does not? Number your answers (a) and (b). [2]

viii. Why did the Dutch sailors think that the hills of Easter Island were sand dunes? [1]

ix. Apart from their height, why do you think the writer compares the stone statues on Easter Island to 'Amsterdam houses'? [1]

x. Why did Captain Cook conclude that Easter Island was desolate? [1]

xi. What kind of 'tackle' do you think would have been needed to build the stone statues? [1]

xii. Expain fully the 'riddle' of Easter Island. [2]

xiii. What did experts use to prove that Easter Island was once 'well-watered and green? [1]

[*Total: 16 marks*]

Chapter **15**

Selecting and retrieving information by lifting

Now we will look at some of the other questions asked at the start of Chapter 3:

- Do I need to use my own words?
- Am I allowed to use words of the original text?

The answer to these questions is that you may use the words of the original text unless you are told otherwise. In questions where you are required to use your own words, the wording of the question will make that clear. You will look at such questions later. Right now you will deal only with questions where you are allowed to use the words of the text. This is called lifting from the text. So you have learned that, unless the question specifies use of own words, it is acceptable to lift from the text.

However, when you lift from the text to answer a question, you must make sure that you do not include material from the text which is not necessary in your answer. If you do include extra, unnecessary information, you could fail to score the available mark. Look at the short passage below:

The appearance of land at the end of a long sea voyage must be a welcome sight for any ship's captain. Yet he has to be particularly alert at this stage of the voyage, for in many parts of the world there are often rocky islands close to the shore he is approaching.

Question: At what stage of a sea journey must a captain be 'particularly alert'?

Answer 1: He must be alert at the end of the voyage.

Answer 2: He must be alert when land appears.

Answer 3: The appearance of land at the end of a long sea voyage.

Answer 4: The appearance of land at the end of a long sea voyage must be a welcome sight for any ship's captain.

Answers 1 and 2 are correct. Each of them had selected and retrieved key words from the passage which answer the question and recast them in a sentence.

Answer 3 is also correct. It is a direct lift from the passage but this is acceptable because, unless otherwise stated, this is not an own words question. This is a literal comprehension question and the answer lies on the surface of the text. It would have been better if the answer had been given in a short sentence but that does not prevent the mark being given.

However, Answer 4 is incorrect because, although it lifts the correct answer, it goes on to lift so much of the text that the question is not in fact answered. This answer does not give 'a stage of a journey' but a lifted sentence which does not answer the question.

So you have learned that, although it is acceptable to lift from the text in answering a question, you must be careful that what you lift does not include extra information which might distort your answer or prevent the question being answered.

Exercise 1   Coral Reefs

From the passage which follows answer the questions by lifting.

A thriving coral reef is one of the most glorious sights on our planet. Anyone swimming underwater near a coral reef for the first time is likely to find it a beautiful place teeming with life of every description set among a rich and random pattern of colours. Coral reefs are second only to rain forests in the huge number of plants and animals they support. Just as forest plants have been used for hundreds of years for medicinal purposes by people living in the rain forests, so some reef plants and animals have been used by people in coastal communities to help cure diseases like malaria.

---

i.   Why does the writer describe coral reefs as 'one of the most glorious sights on our planet'?   [1]

ii. In what ways are coral reefs almost as important as rain forests?   [1]

iii. What common benefit do people living in rain forests and people living near coral reefs get from local plants?   [1]

[*Total: 3 marks*]

Exercise 2 Grandfather

From the passage which follows answer the questions by lifting.

She loved to sit on her grandfather's knee while he read her stories for what seemed like hours. He never tired of reading to her and it would never have occurred to her that he would refuse to do so. His voice was gruff but comforting; it was his reading voice just for her. Sometimes she took a peek at his face; his skin was wrinkly and she liked to trace with her eye particular lines as they meandered from one side of his face to the other. He had a white, bushy moustache which curled up at the edges and twitched as his lips moved over the mysterious symbols on the page which she did not understand but loved to listen to. She had to sit very still as his clothes were scratchy and made her legs red if she move too much.

> i.   Why did the little girl like to sit on her grandfather's knee?   [1]
>
> ii. What one feature of her grandfather's voice might have been
>   frightening to the little girl?   [1]
>
> iii. Apart from the moustache, what was it about her grandfather's
>   face which interested the little girl?   [1]
>
> iv. Why did the little girl have to sit very still on her grandfather's
>   knee?   [1]
>
> [*Total: 4 marks*]

Exercise 3 Jennifer

From the passage which follows answer the questions by lifting.

She spent a day with an old friend and felt really refreshed. She and Jennifer as a team had a long history. They made their shy introductions on their first day at primary school and since then have shared many high – and low – points in their respective lives. They joined the local youth club together, and walked and talked and went shopping together. They discussed each other's boyfriends. In a nutshell they grew up together. Her day with Jennifer restored her well-being, her happiness, her sanity. But more that that, it made her reflect on the nature of real friendship – having someone value you for what you are.

i.   What had made the woman feel 'really refreshed'?   [1]

ii. When did the woman and her friend meet each other for the first
     time?   [1]

iii. Give an example of one activity that the two friends did together. [1]

iv. What was the main advantage gained by the woman in her day
     spent with her old friend?   [1]

                                                        [*Total: 4 marks*]

Exercise 4   Chris

From the passage which follows answer the questions by lifting.

Chris's best friend had told him he was mad even to consider running the
London marathon, and, as his friend was a doctor, Chris took his comment
seriously. However, for months he was out running on the pavements around
his home trying to forget that his build was neither slim nor athletic. Not for
him the lure of fame or fortune; he had committed himself to raise money for
charity. More than twenty six miles – he told himself not to think about it as
he sweated on the treadmill in his local gym. He tried – unsuccessfully – to
think of it as fun, but that was stretching his imagination too far. But when it
was over Chris did feel just that little superior – and he had had a great tour
of London!

i.   Why did Chris take his friend's comments seriously?   [1]

ii. What two reasons does the writer give to suggest that Chris was
     not suited to running a marathon?   [1]

iii. Why was Chris determined to run the marathon?   [1]

iv. In what two ways did Chris train for the marathon?   [2]

v.   Apart from making Chris feel superior, what was the other
     advantage to him of running the marathon?   [1]

                                                        [*Total: 5 marks*]

Although all of these questions can be answered by lifting, they could be answered in other ways. But the important point here is that, although some questions can be answered by lifting, you must not copy sections of the text which do not in fact answer the questions. As Examiners say, in such cases, the excess in your answer denies the mark. It tends to be easier, literal comprehension questions which can be answered by lifting.

So you have learned that, when you answer a question by lifting, it is important to make sure that you do not stray into areas of the text that are irrelevant to the correct answer to the question you are answering.

Chapter

More exercises in lifting

For each of the exercises which follow:

- Read the passage carefully twice.

- Answer the questions by lifting. Do not try to use own words at this stage.

- Answer the questions in sentences, but do not waste time copying out question stems.

- Be careful that what you lift does not include extra information which might distort your answer or prevent the question being answered.

Exercise 1   Grandfather's Study

In Grandfather's study, mounted butterflies and moths had disintegrated into small heaps of iridescent dust that powdered the bottom of their glass display cases, leaving the pins that had impaled them. Cruel. The room was rank with fungus and disease.

Rahel (on a stool, on top of a table) rummaged in a book cupboard with dull, dirty glass panes. Her bare footprints were clear in the dust on the floor. They led from the door to the table (dragged to the bookshelf) to the stool (dragged to the table and lifted onto it). She was looking for something.

On the top shelf, the leather binding of grandfather's set of 'The Insect Wealth of India' had lifted off each book and buckled like corrugated asbestos. Insects tunnelled through the pages, burrowing arbitrarily from species to species, turning organised information into yellow lace.

Rahel groped behind the row of books and brought out hidden things. A smooth seashell and a spiky one. A plastic case for contact lenses. An orange pipette.

Behind the books, Rahel's puzzled fingers encountered something else. Another magpie had had the same idea. She brought it out and wiped the dust off with the sleeve of her shirt. It was a flat packet wrapped in clear plastic and stuck with Sellotape. A scrap of white paper inside it said 'Esthappen and Rahel'. In Ammu's writing. There were four tattered notebooks in it.

Source: *The God of Small Things* by Arundhati Roy, Harper Collins Publishers Ltd

   i. What had happened to Grandfather's collection of moths? [1]

  ii. Where in the study had Grandfather kept his collection of moths? [1]

 iii. Apart from the dead moths, what else about the study might have made Rahel dislike it? [1]

 iv. The cupboard had 'dirty glass panes'. What else was dirty? [1]

  v. How had Rahel got the table to the bookshelf? [1]

 vi. How had Rahel got the stool on to the table? [1]

 vii. Explain fully what had happened to Grandfather's set of books entitled 'The Insect Wealth of India'. [2]

viii. What did Rahel have to do to retrieve the 'hidden things'? [1]

 ix. Explain fully how you can tell that the notebooks were important to Ammu. [2]

[Total: 11 marks]

Exercise 2   The Brazilian Rain Forest

Once a year the skies of western Brazil grow dark by day as well as by night. Farmers and cattle owners burn down vast areas of the great rain forests around the river Amazon to clear land for crop-growing and cattle rearing. Smoke from the fires blots out the sun. Scientists, now keenly aware of the dangers to the earth's environment, see this great annual destruction as a major peril for Brazil, and also for the rest of the world. Politicians have joined scientists to try to stop the foolish waste of the precious resources of the planet.

For more than four hundred years settlers and farmers have been attacking Brazil's forests in one way or another. They tried to snatch land for themselves from the seemingly indestructible jungles, but their power of recovery defeated their efforts. New trees continually filled in the small patches of land that they cleared. Nowadays, modern machinery can cut down trees at an alarming speed, and the controlled burning down of the forests has meant that areas larger than some whole countries have been permanently stripped bare. One result of this destruction is becoming alarmingly obvious. The forests contain an astonishing variety of animal and plant life which is slowly but surely disappearing. One type of tree may maintain more than four hundred insect species, each square kilometre of forest its own assortment of birds and mammals.

i. Once a year, what is unusual about the skies of Western Brazil? [1]

ii. Why do farmers and cattle owners burn down the forests? [1]

iii. In the first paragraph, what evidence does the writer give to suggest that vast areas are burned? [1]

iv. Explain fully why scientists are worried about the burning of the forests. [2]

v. How can you tell that politicians agree with scientists? [1]

vi. Is the destruction of the forests a new phenomenon? Give a reason for your answer. [1]

vii. What feature of the jungles meant that settlers were unable 'to snatch land for themselves', and what evidence of this feature does the writer give to support his claim? [2]

viii. In the second paragraph, what evidence does the writer give to suggest that vast areas are burned? [1]

ix. Apart from burning down forests, how else is land obtained for farmers and cattle owners? [1]

x. What is 'one result' of the destruction of the forests? [1]

[*Total: 12 marks*]

Exercise 3   Estha and Rahel

They were nearly born on a bus, Estha and Rahel. The car in which Baba, their father, was taking Ammu, their mother, to hospital in Shillong to have them, broke down on the winding tea estate road. They abandoned the car and flagged down a crowded State Transport bus. With the queer compassion of the very poor for the comparatively well off, or perhaps only because they saw how hugely pregnant Ammu was, seated passengers made room for the couple and for the rest of the journey Estha and Rahel's father had to hold their mother's wobbling stomach (with them in it) to prevent it from wobbling.

According to Estha, if they'd been born on the bus, they'd have got free bus rides for the rest of their lives. It wasn't clear where he'd got this information from, or how he knew these things, but for years the twins harboured a faint resentment against their parents for having diddled them out of a lifetime of free bus rides.

They also believed that if they were killed on a zebra crossing, they'd have got free bus rides for the rest of their lives. They had the definite impression that that was what zebra crossings were meant for. Free funerals. Of course there were no zebra crossings to get killed on in Ayamenem, or, for that matter, even in Kottayam, which was the nearest town, but they'd seen some from the car window when they went to Cochin, which was a two hour drive away.

Source: *The God of Small Things* by Arundhanti Roy, Harper Collins Publishers Ltd

i. Where were Estha and Rahel's parents going when their car broke down?	[1]
ii. How did they complete their journey after the car broke down?	[1]
iii. Why might we be surprised that the passengers on the bus felt sorry for Baba and Ammu?	[1]
iv. Why might we expect the passengers on the bus to feel sorry for Baba and Ammu?	[1]
v. Why did Baba have to hold Ammu's stomach on the bus journey?	[1]
vi. What did Estha think would have happened if he and his sister had been born on the bus?	[1]
vii. How did Estha know what would have happened if he and his sister had been born on the bus?	[1]
viii. Why did the twins feel resentful towards their parents?	[1]
ix. According to the twins, what was the advantage of being killed on a zebra crossing?	[1]
x. Why were the twins unlikely to be killed on a zebra crossing?	[1]

[*Total: 10 marks*]

Exercise 4   The Domestication of Animals

There are thousands of species of wild animals, and yet surprisingly few, for example the goat and the cow, have been domesticated. The reason is that it takes special qualities to make animals suitable for domestication. They must be strong enough to withstand removal from their mother at an early age and find food for themselves so that her milk can be used for human consumption. They must breed freely in captivity – a guarantee that the farmer has a living – and be easy to look after. Domestic or farm animals must be able to develop a liking for man, enjoy comfort, and accept confinement and control. And, of course, they must be useful: primarily as a source of food, but also in the provision of wool or hide for clothing and sometimes as a means of transport or pulling power.

Animals suitable for domestication only emerged with the spread of grass. Millions of years ago, the world's rainfall decreased, forests diminished, low-growing plants appeared, then grass, and, with them, grazing animals developed. Thus sheep and antelope appeared on the scene, followed by cows, goats and horses. Not until about 10,000 years ago did man develop the idea of taking animals into captivity. There was wild game in abundance, so what prompted the idea?

It could have come naturally from his experience as a nomadic hunter. As he followed his prey on their yearly migrations he gradually began to influence their movements and behaviour in certain situations. For example, some animals would be driven into a narrow, steep-sided valley where they could more easily be rounded up and some of them slaughtered. Or perhaps the idea arose out of keeping young animals as pets. Predators trying to steal food from the hunters' camp were fed by the men and encouraged to become part of the community: the predator changed into the pet.

i.   Why might we be surprised that few species of animals have
     been domesticated?   [1]

ii. Why are domestic animals taken from their mothers at an early
     age?   [1]

iii. Why do animals removed from their mothers at an early age have
     to be strong?   [1]

iv. What must happen to ensure that the farmer makes a living?   [1]

v. What are the three uses to which domestic animals can be put? Number your answers (a), (b) and (c). [3]

vi. What is the main reason for the development of domestic animals? [1]

vii. What two things happened after the forests diminished which led to grazing animals? Number your answers (a) and (b). [2]

viii. According to the writer, why might we be surprised that man started to take animals into captivity? [1]

ix. What did early man do which shows he was a 'nomadic hunter'? [1]

x. What was the advantage of driving animals into a 'narrow, steep-sided valley'? [1]

xi. Why did men feed predators which were trying to steal their food? [1]

[*Total: 14 marks*]

Chapter **17**

Evaluating information

You have already seen that Assessment Objective (v) in 'O' Level English Language is to select, retrieve, evaluate and combine information. You dealt with selection and retrieval in the previous chapters. Now you will move on to evaluation of information. When you evaluate anything, you weigh it up and consider its importance in relation to other things. In an evaluation question, you go beyond merely selecting and retrieving the information required to answer the question.

Go back to the questions asked at the start of Chapter 13:

- Do I need to use my own words?

We have already established that the answer to this question is that you may use the words of the text unless the question tells you specifically not to. In cases where you are required to answer in your own words, the question wording will make that clear. Own words questions go beyond merely selecting and retrieving information. This does not mean that you do not have to begin by selecting and retrieving the necessary information – it is in fact important to do so. But there is a further stage in answering such questions, which is to render the key words selected and retrieved into words which do not come from the text.

Example 1

In time, our early ancestors came to rely a great deal on communicating knowledge to one another. This enabled them to find more food.

Question: Using your own words, say what enabled our ancestors to become superior to many other animals in finding food.

Step 1 in answering this question is to identify it as an own words question. This is not difficult as the question wording makes it quite clear that you are required to answer in your own words. Such questions will always be clearly signposted in an examination paper – there are no tricks here! Similarly, you must realise that, if you do not use your own words, you are wasting your time. You will gain no marks for lifting in an own words question.

Step 2 in answering this question is to select and retrieve the key words. The key words are the words you are required to re-cast in words or expressions of your own. Careful reading of the text should lead you to select and retrieve 'communicating' and 'knowledge' as the key words.

Step 3 in answering this question is to evaluate the key words you have selected and retrieved. If this were not an own words question, selection and retrieval would be sufficient. But in an own words question you must go a little further and evaluate these key words, which means that you must weigh up their meaning in the text and come up with synonyms or other equivalents.

So your synonyms for 'communicate' might be 'pass on', 'tell', 'share' or 'inform', while your synonyms for 'knowledge' might be 'information', 'what they had learned' or 'what they had found out'.

Your answer might be: They passed on to one another what they had found out.

Notice that we established that own words questions ask for synonyms or other equivalents. You do not need to give a single word to re-cast a single word. Nor do you need to give the same part of speech, i.e. a noun for an noun or a verb for a verb. So 'what they had learned' is a perfect answer to re-cast 'knowledge' although it is not a single word answer. However, 'what they know' would not be an acceptable answer because 'know' is a derivative of 'knowledge' which means that it comes from the same family.

So you have learned that, in an own words question, a single word synonym is not necessary for a correct answer. However, you will get no credit for answering in a derivative of the key word.

Example 2

The construction of the lighthouse began in 1895 and, because of the island's isolated location and hostile weather, it took four years to complete.

Question: Why did it take four years to build the lighthouse? Answer in your own words.

Step 1: This is an own words question.

Step 2: Key words are 'isolated' and 'hostile'.

Step 3: Possible synonyms for 'isolated' are 'far away', 'lonely', 'separated', 'cut off'. Possible synonyms for 'hostile' are 'unkind', 'inclement', 'nasty', 'bad'.

Answer: It took four years to build because the island was far away and because of bad weather.

Exercise 1

Answer the own words questions attached to the short passages below.

i. 'When Jennifer stepped from the car, she was horrified at the scene of devastation before her.' [2]

In your own words, explain how Jennifer felt when she stepped from the car, and the reason why she felt this way. [2]

ii. 'The rush hour traffic crawled along the road, smoke billowing from exhaust pipes.'

In your own words, describe the rush hour traffic. [2]

iii. 'Undoubtedly, the reduction in government spending on education will lead to a deterioration in literacy.' [2]

According to the writer, what will be the result of the reduction in government spending on education? Answer in your own words.

iv. 'The creepers grew in profusion around the house, and even coiled round the window sills.' [2]

Explain in your own words what the writer tells us about the creepers. [2]

v. 'In the past, governments have sometimes taken strong action to preserve an environment which has been threatened. Unfortunately, these governments have often disregarded the views of the people living there.' [2]

Using your own words, explain what mistakes were made, according to the writer, by governments in the past which tried to preserve an environment which had been threatened.

vi. 'Speed boats take tourists every day out to the coral reefs. This leads to the inevitable destruction of the reefs.' [2]

According to the writer, what is the result of tourists' speed boat trips to the coral reefs? Answer in your own words. [2]

vii. 'With mounting astonishment, the captain saw that there was nobody in or around the lighthouse.'

What was the captain's reaction to the fact that there was nobody in or around the lighthouse? Answer in your own words. [2]

viii. 'Speeding downhill on a bicycle is an experience which is both exhilarating and terrifying.'

Explain in your own words how the writer describes the experience of speeding downhill on a bicycle. [2]

ix. 'Even today, coral reefs are still essential to people living in the tropics, whether used to manufacture tools or simply to adorn their houses.'

Why are coral reefs still essential to people living in the tropics? Answer in your own words. [2]

x. 'It seems likely that, in the future, schemes for the protection of coral reefs will be initiated and supervised by local people.'

In your own words, explain the part that is likely to be played by local people in schemes for the protection of coral reefs. [2]

[*Total : 20 Marks*]

Exercise 2

Read the passage below and answer the own words questions which follow.

Out of all the huts the villagers were reluctantly emerging – the children first, inquisitive rather than frightened. The men and women had the air of people already condemned by authority. They stared at the ground and waited.

The Lieutenant barked out: 'Anyone who shelters the traitor is himself a traitor.' Their immobility seemed to anger him. Furious, he raised his voice. 'You're fools if you still believe what he tells you.'

Source: *The Power and the Glory* by Graham Greene, Penguin Books

i. In your own words, explain the effect the arrival of the lieutenant had on the children. [2]

ii. What had made the Lieutenant 'furious'? Answer in your own words. [1]

[*Total: 3 Marks*]

Signposts in own words questions

Just as we saw that there are signposts in inferential questions, in the same way there are signposts in own words questions. The obvious signpost is that the question asks you to use your own words. However, a more subtle signpost might be a quotation from the passage. This quotation might be a single word, an expression or even a whole sentence. (In the last question, the quotation signpost was the word 'furious'.) Quotations can be signposts which direct you to the area of text where you will find the key words, i.e. the words which you have to select, retrieve and evaluate so that you can put them into your own words.

So you have learned that, if you are given quotation signposts in own words questions, you should use them to help you to find the key words, i.e. the words you will have to put into your own words.

Exercise 3

Read the passage below and answer the own words question which follows.

There was a large rent in the mattress; he pulled out a handful of straw and put his fingers in again. The man gazed out with false indifference at the public gardens, the dark mud- banks and the masts of sailing ships; the lightning flapped behind them and the thunder came nearer.

Source: *The Power and the Glory* by Graham Greene, Penguin Books

i. In your own words, describe the man's attitude to his surroundings.

[2 marks]

Exercise 4

Read the passage below and answer the own words questions which follow.

Once the newspapers got hold of the story, there was much speculation, most of it unconvincing. The mystery has never been conclusively solved, but for over a century many explanations as to what happened have been suggested. One theory is that violence broke out and one of the lighthouse keepers murdered his colleagues and threw them over the cliff; he then jumped over the cliff himself through shame at what he had done. A second, less fanciful, theory is that two of the men got up early to repair the devastation of a night of particularly inclement weather.

i. According to the writer, what happened 'once the newspapers got
    hold of the story'? Answer in your own words.   [2]

ii. The mystery 'has never been conclusively solved'. Explain in your
     own words what this means.   [2]

iii. The second theory as to what happened is 'less fanciful'. Explain
      in your own words what this means.   [2]

iv. According to the second theory, why did two of the men get up
     early? Answer in your own words.   [3]

[*Total: 9 marks*]

Exercise 5

Read the passage below and answer the own words questions which follow.

As communities grew and developed, the greater the variety of goods there
was to inspect for bartering. So it became more and more difficult to decide
what one thing was worth compared with another. Eventually, a very basic
form of money appeared, often things such as knives, sword or axe-heads,
made in a small size. Being fashioned out of metal, they had a special value,
since it required a good deal of labour to extract them from the earth.
Eventually, a currency emerged which would remain popular for a very long
time and over a wide area, and that was the cowrie shell. What made cowrie
shells a unique form of currency was they defied any sort of imitation. However,
cowrie shells were shipped abroad in increasingly large quantities. This meant
that through time their value as money was diminished.

i. According to the writer, what happened 'as communities grew
    and developed'? Answer in your own words.   [2]

ii. Explain in your own words the reason why metal objects acquired
     a 'special value' as money.   [2]

iii. What made cowrie shells a reliable form of money? Answer in
      your own words.   [2]

iv. 'Cowrie shells were shipped abroad 'in increasingly large quantities'.
     Explain in your own words what this means.   [2]

v. What happened to cowrie shells 'through time'? Answer in your own words. [2]

[*Total: 10 marks*]

Now we will deal with the last of the questions asked at the start of Chapter 13:
Is the question asking only about the story or argument of the text?
Is the question asking about particular features of language, e.g. figures of speech?

Chapter **18**

More exercises in own words questions

You saw in the previous chapter that some questions ask for answers which are not lifted from the text but are to be expressed in your own words. You are to evaluate the language of the passage and re-cast it in language of your own. We will use some material you have seen already.

For each of the exercises which follow:

- Read the passage carefully twice.
- Pick out the key words which you are being asked to re-cast in own words.
- Find other ways of expressing the key words. You may be able to do this with a single synonym but you are allowed to use more than one word provided you show understanding.

Exercise 1 Pavlo

Half-way along the fence was a cluster of glossy green plants and our pet monkey Pavlo liked to lie under them to keep warm, hiding from the big white cat next door, for this beast was obviously under the impression that Pavlo was a strange type of rat which she had to kill. She liked to spend hours stalking him, but, since she was as conspicuous as a ball of snow among the plants, she never managed to catch Pavlo unawares. Pavlo lived with us for eight years. When he died, the house and garden seemed empty without his tiny presence. Even the white cat next door seemed depressed, for without Pavlo in it our garden had lost its appeal for her. Pavlo was a particularly attractive pet, and we mourned the loss not only of his quirky personality but also of his affectionate nature.

i.   What did the cat like to do with Pavlo and why was she never successful? Answer in your own words. [2]

ii. Explain in your own words why the cat seemed depressed when Pavlo died. [1]

iii. What did the family find so attractive about Pavlo? Answer in your own words. [2]

[*Total: 5 marks*]

Exercise 2 Man And Animals

The hunter feared and admired the animals he pursued for their strength, speed and superior powers of sight, hearing and scent. Later this respect became a kind of worship. As man tamed and farmed certain species, however, a relationship of mutual affection developed.

i. In your own words, explain the three reasons for man's fear and admiration for the animals he pursued. [3]

ii. What happened 'as man tamed and farmed certain species'? Answer in your own words. [3]

[*Total: 6 marks*]

Exercise 3 The Ruined Books

On the top shelf, the leather binding of Grandfather's set of 'The Insect Wealth of India' had lifted off each book and buckled. Insects tunnelled through the pages, burrowing arbitrarily from species to species, turning organised information into yellow lace.

Source: *The God of Small Things* by Arundhati Roy, Harper Collins Publishers Ltd

i. In your own words, explain what had happened to the leather binding of Grandfather's books. [2]

ii. The insects were 'burrowing arbitrarily' through the pages of the books. Explain in your own words what this means. [2]

[*Total: 4 marks*]

Exercise 4 Forest Destruction

For more than four hundred years settlers and farmers have been attacking Brazil's forests in one way or another. They tried to snatch land for themselves from the seemingly indestructible jungles, but their power of recovery defeated their efforts. Nowadays, modern machinery can cut down trees at an alarming speed, and the controlled burning down of the forests has meant that areas larger than some whole countries have been permanently stripped bare.

One result of this destruction is becoming alarmingly obvious. The forests contain an astonishing variety of animal and plant life which is slowly but surely disappearing.

i. Apart from their 'power of recovery', what other feature of the jungles would have made the settlers' task of taking land for themselves very difficult? Answer in your own words. [2]

ii. In your own words, explain what the burning down has done to large areas of forests. [3]

iii. The forests contain 'an astonishing variety' of animal and plant life. Explain in your own words what this means. [2]

[*Total: 7 marks*]

Exercise 5   How Animals Became Pets

Domestic or farm animals must be able to develop a liking for man, enjoy comfort, and accept confinement and control. Not until about 10,000 years ago did man develop the idea of taking animals into captivity. There was wild game in abundance, so what prompted the idea?

It could have come naturally from his experience as a nomadic hunter. As he followed his prey on their yearly migrations he gradually began to influence their movements and behaviour in certain situations. Or perhaps the idea arose out of the keeping of young animals as pets. Predators trying to steal food from the hunters' camp were fed by the men and encouraged to become part of the community: the predator changed into the pet.

i. According to the writer, domestic animals must have a liking for man and enjoy comfort. In your own words, explain what other features are necessary. [3]

ii. In your own words, explain what gradual effect man had on animals in certain situations as he 'followed their yearly migrations'. [4]

iii. 'The predator changed into the pet.' Explain in your own words what this means. [2]

[*Total: 9 marks*]

Exercise 6   Sharing the Earth

Today, zoologists and naturalists are alarmed by the rapid disappearance of many species of wild life due to the ruthless exploitation of the land by man for his needs, resulting in the destruction of forests and plains. These experts study animals scientifically and form societies and pressure groups to protect them and their habitats. Conflicting attitudes need to be reconciled if man is to continue sharing the earth in harmony with the animals.

> i. According to the writer, what alarms zoologists and naturalists today? Answer in your own words. [3]
>
> ii. Man is guilty of 'ruthless exploitation'. Explain in your own words what this means. [2]
>
> iii. In your own words, explain what needs to happen, according to the writer, if man is to 'continue sharing the earth in harmony with the animals'. [3]
>
> [*Total: 8 marks*]

Exercise 7 Venice

(Venice has recently been flooded and long term damage has been done to the city.)

As soon as Venice's peril was fully realised, there were endless conferences and tours of inspection. Plans have been drawn up to preserve Venice, but little action has followed. A special law was passed to save the city, but not implemented. Foreign organisations collected and sent to Italy great sums of money for the same purpose, but this money was taxed by the Italian government. Governments rose and fell; committees were formed and disbanded. Scientists, technicians and art specialists did experiments and made recommendations. The government ignored them all. Those who had the power to save Venice were not prepared to take responsibility for their decisions: those who were prepared to take responsibility did not have the power.

Venice, probably in a more tragic way than anywhere else, poses a question Western society is reluctant to face: how much of its present wealth is it prepared to sacrifice to conserve the glories of the past?

> i. 'Venice's peril was fully realised'. Explain in your own words what this means. [3]
>
> ii. Explain in your own words what happened 'as soon as Venice's peril was fully realised'. [4]
>
> iii. Although 'a special law was passed to save the city', why was it unsuccessful? Answer in your own words. [1]

iv. Explain in your own words what is meant by 'governments rose and fell'. [2]

v. How successful were committees in saving Venice? Answer in your own words. [2]

vi. What contribution to the saving of Venice did scientists, technicians and art specialists make? Answer in your own words. [2]

vii. Those who 'had power to save Venice' failed to do so. Explain in your words why they failed. [3]

viii. The writer is clearly critical of Western society's attitude to 'the glories of the past'. Explain in your own words what he is criticising. [3]

[*Total: 20 marks*]

Exercise 8   The Ferry Boat

(The crew have lost control of a ferry boat and there is the danger that the boat might sink.)

The chief engineer decide to ignore instructions from the captain and to dock the boat himself with the aid of the dockers whom he could see through his open door. As he did so, there was a rush of passengers to the boat's rails. Those who would not risk their lives by jumping on to the quay ran from side to side of the deck in a frenzy of impatience, creating an alarming instability in the vessel. Finally, the bow-gate clanged down on to the ramp and the remaining passengers scrambled thankfully ashore.

Throughout all this, there was only one calm place in view. On the car deck of the ferry there was a new police truck. The policemen inside it, in their crisp uniforms, ignored the surrounding panic. They sat upright and gazed straight ahead through the spotless glass, while the passengers scrambled around their vehicle. All correct they sat, not a scratch on their paintwork, not a crease in their uniforms out of line, like new toys on a shop shelf. Attached to their windscreen was a little sticker – 'This is a wide-zone toughened windscreen' – which recalled the world of accident prevention and road safety. But what of the correct procedure in the event of approaching a quay too fast? This must have seemed as remote from the world they controlled as rescue must have seemed to the occupants of an earlier ferry which had overturned in midstream while nobody noticed. The last person to leave the boat was a grey-faced man with a bandaged head. He stumbled off as he had stumbled on, and the police drove past him unhurriedly, models of detachment and moderation.

i. Passengers were in 'a frenzy of impatience'. Explain in your own words what this means. [2]

ii. In your own words, explain what was the effect on the ferry of the passengers running from side to side. [3]

ii. How did the passengers behave when 'the bow gate clanged down on to the ramp'? Answer in your own words. [2]

iv. The policemen 'ignored the surrounding panic'. Explain in your own words what this means. [3]

v. In your own words, explain how you can tell from their actions that the policemen were ignoring the 'surrounding panic'. [2]

vi. According to the writer, what was the attitude of the policemen to safety procedure in the event of a ferry 'approaching a quay too fast'? Answer in your own words. [2]

vii. In your own words, explain what happened to the 'earlier ferry'. [3]

viii. The policemen were 'models of detachment and moderation'. Explain in your own words what this means. [3]

[*Total: 20 marks*]

Chapter

Combining information

We have already seen that Assessment Objective (v) in 'O' Level English Language is to select, retrieve, evaluate and combine information from written texts. We have already worked on selection, retrieval and evaluation. Now it is time to look at combining information.

When you are given questions which require you to combine information, you must follow the normal procedures for selection and retrieval, and possibly for evaluation. What makes combining questions different from other types of questions is that in a combining question you will be required to give more than one piece of information in order to answer the question properly.

Signposts of combining questions

The most obvious signpost of a question which requires you to give more than one answer is the question which asks for two reasons. We have already encountered such questions in earlier chapters.

A more subtle type of combining question is the question which asks you to answer fully. The word 'fully' often suggests that there is more than one angle to the answer. That might mean that there are two separate answers, or it might mean that, although strictly speaking there is only one answer, that answer has sufficient depth that there will be a more obvious answer on the surface of the text and a less accessible answer underneath the text. Or it might mean that you are required to elaborate on your basic answer in order to score the marks available for the answer.

Another signpost of combining questions is the number of marks allocated to the answer. The mark allocation at the end of a question is there to help you, not to help your teacher or some other examiner. It is obvious that a question which carries two or more marks is more difficult than a question which carries only one mark. If the question is allocated two marks, that is a code for you, telling you that this question might have two distinct answers, or a depth or elaboration to the more basic answer.

Example 1

The sun beat down on the pavements of the town. It was home to three thousand or so inhabitants, with its quaint little market stalls selling hot food, its winding streets and crowded shops. Outside the town, boys played on the banks of the dried-up river.

> **Question**: How can you tell that the weather is hot? Give two reasons for your answer. *[2 marks]*

Answer 1: I know it is hot because the sun beat down on the pavements and because the river had dried up.

Answer 2: I know it is hot because the sun beat down on the pavements of the town and because the market stall were selling hot food.

Answer 3: I know it is hot because the sun beat down on the pavements of the town. It was home to three thousand or so inhabitants. Outside the town, boys played on the banks of the river. The river was dried up.

Answer 4: I know it is hot because, firstly, the sun beat down on the pavements of the town and the town was home to three thousand or so inhabitants. Secondly, the river was dried up.

Exercise 1

Working with a partner, decide which mark should be allocated to each of the examples above, giving reasons for the mark decided. You should have something like this:

Answer 1 scores 2 marks. Both answers are clearly stated, namely that the sun was beating down on the pavements, and that the river was dried up. It might have clarified the answer if it had been divided into (i) and (ii), but the answer is sufficiently clear. Two answers were asked for, and two answers were given.

Answer 2 scores 1 mark. The first answer is correct, namely that the sun beat down on the pavements, but the second answer is incorrect. The answer has merely made a wrong response to the word 'hot' in the question and automatically linked it to the word 'hot' in the text. Hot food has nothing to do with hot weather.

Answer 3 scores 1 mark. Although both reasons are given for recognising that the weather is hot, this answer actually offer four reasons. In such cases, only the first two answers are looked at. To offer more than two answers to a question which asks for two reasons is to offend the rubric, as Examiners say. In other words, the answer does not give what the question asked for. In this particular example, the first reason offered is that the sun beat down on the pavements, which is correct. The second reason offered is that the town was home to three thousand or so inhabitants, which is incorrect. The third and fourth reasons would not even be considered in an examination.

Answer 4 scores 2 marks. Although the answer is almost identical to answer 3, it divides the reasons into 'firstly' and 'secondly', so that the two reasons, or 'limbs' as they are called by Examiners, are clearly defined. In the first limb, it would be reasonable to conclude that 'the town was home to three thousand or so inhabitants' is extra information rather than an offered reason. We may not like the inclusion of this 'gloss' on the answer, but it would be unfair to deny the mark for the whole limb, because it nevertheless makes the point that the sun was beating down on the pavements.

Example 2

When passing a pet shop in my home town, I saw it contained a cage full of marmoset monkeys, which had to fight for a place to sit. As I watched this pathetic little group, I was moved by pity for all animals in captivity. I felt I had to rescue at least one of these little animals and my heart went out to the smallest one, Pavlo, who was always getting knocked out of the way.

Question: Give two reasons why Pavlo was the marmoset monkey chosen by the writer.   *[2 marks]*

Answer 1: Pavlo was chosen because the writer was moved by pity for all animals in captivity and because his heart went out to the smallest one.

Answer 2: Pavlo was chosen because the writer was moved by pity for all animals in captivity and because his heart went out to the smallest one, Pavlo.

Answer 3: Pavlo was chosen because the writer felt he had to rescue at least one of these little animals, his heart went out to the smallest one, Pavlo, and Pavlo was always getting knocked out of the way.

Answer 4: Pavlo was chosen because, firstly, he was the smallest and, secondly, because he was always getting knocked out of the way.

Exercise 2

Working with a partner, decide which marks should be allocated to each of the examples above, giving reasons for the mark decided. You should have something like this:

Answer 1 scores 0 marks. Being moved by pity for all animals is not specific to Pavlo and therefore does not answer the question. 'His heart went out to the smallest one' is a tempting answer, but it does not spell out that is is Pavlo who is the smallest one.

Answer 2 scores 1 mark. Being moved by pity is not specific to Pavlo and therefore does not answer the question. But the second mark is scored because the answer is specific to Pavlo, i.e. the writer's heart went out to the smallest one, Pavlo.

Answer 3 scores 1 mark, because it offers three limbs and only the first two will be considered. So, 'he felt he had to rescue at least one of these little animals' is incorrect for the first limb, 'his heart went out to the smallest one, Pavlo' scores a mark for the second limb, and the third limb 'Pavlo was always getting knocked out of the way' fails to score, not because it is incorrect, (it is correct) but because it is the third limb offered and only the first two are considered.

Answer 4 scores 2 marks, because it gives two limbs, each of which is correct. The way in which the limbs are separated by 'firstly' and 'secondly' helps to underpin the clarity of the answer.

Example 3

Samir pedalled his new bicycle along the pavement, gathering speed as he went. He suppressed the thought that his mother had told him not to go beyond the end of their street. He was proud of his new bicycle – its shiny wheels, its smart, red frame, its tinkling bell. Perhaps if he went beyond the end of the street, he would see his school friend, Nissar. Nissar had a bicycle and might perhaps be playing with it in his own street. His mother would never find out that he had strayed into forbidden territory. Along he went, further and further. Then he remembered his mother's anger the last time he had disobeyed her – it just wasn't worth it. He pulled on the brakes and reluctantly turned the bicycle back in the direction of his house.

Question: Explain fully why Samir decided not to go any further on his bicycle. [2]

Answer 1 He decided not to go any further because his mother had told him not to go beyond the end of his street.

Answer 2 He decided not to go any further because his mother had told him not to go beyond the end of their street and because he was proud of his new bicycle.

Answer 3 He decided not to go any further because his mother had told him not to go beyond the end of their street and because he remembered her anger the last time he had disobeyed her.

Answer 4 He decided not to go any further because he suppressed the thought that his mother had told him not to go beyond the end of their street and because he remembered how angry she had been the last time he disobeyed her. It just wasn't worth it.

Exercise 3

Working with a partner, decide what mark should be allocated to each of the examples above, giving reasons for the mark decided. You should have something like this:

Answer 1 scores 1 mark because it gives a correct answer. Samir decided to go no further because his mother had forbidden it. However, this answer fails to take into account the word 'fully' in the question, which indicates either a two part answer or an answer with more depth than a question to which one mark only is allocated.

Answer 2 scores 1 mark because, although it responds to the word 'fully' in the question, and takes account of the fact that either a two part answer is required or an answer with more depth than a one mark question, it merely give the first two elements of the paragraph, the second of which is irrelevant to the question. The fact that he was proud of his new bicycle is not a reason to turn back; indeed, it would probably make him want to continue. Answer 2 does not sift through the entire paragraph to look for depth.

Answer 3 scores 2 marks, because it gives the reason that Samir decided to turn back because his mother had forbidden him to go beyond the end of their street. But the answer also responds to the two mark allocation of the question, and the word 'fully' in it, and gives the idea that Samir remembered his mother's anger the last time he had disobeyed her. Either fear of punishment, or fear of upsetting his mother, is the depth to the answer. This answer goes beyond the simple statement that his mother had forbidden him to go beyond a certain point.

Answer 4 scores 1 mark because it is not sufficiently focused in its first section. The point is not made that Samir went no further because his mother had forbidden it. In fact, by merely copying out 'he suppressed the thought that his mother had told him not to go beyond the end of their street', the answer is actually stating the opposite of the correct answer. He is not remembering what his mother had told him because he is deliberately putting it out of his mind. The second mark is scored with reference to the fact that he remembered his mother's anger the last time he had disobeyed her. By adding 'it just wasn't worth it' the answer is still valid, because the final sentence does not make nonsense oes not of the sentence which comes before it; it is merely an extra piece of information.

Exercise 4   Pompeii

Read the passage and answer the combining question which follows.

In the middle years of the first century AD, Pompeii was a prosperous and thriving city, only a few days' journey by road from the great city of Rome. It had about 20,000 residents, and was situated on a well-watered coast plain with particularly fertile soil bearing three or more crops a year. The climate was gentle, with brief winters, long springs and autumns, and summer days cooled by sea breezes.

i. Give three reasons why the coastal plain around Pompeii could bear three or more crops a year'. [3 marks]

Exercise 5   The Rhinoceros

Read the passage and answer the combining question which follows.

Up ahead, the leading ranger had halted and was looking intently to his left. Then he started to run very fast to his right. Immediately his well-disciplined and heavily armed companions dispersed.

Everyone ran as fast as he could, though where to or what from it was impossible to tell. The leading ranger pointed his rifle towards a bush from which there slowly emerged a rhinoceros. The ranger dropped his rifle and ran. I dived behind a thorn bush and for five minutes I watched as the rhinoceros chased eight men around its territory. Equipment was dropped: notebooks, a box of dates, a canvas bucket, items of clothing, even some of the rifles.

> i. The writer describes the men as 'well-disciplined'. Give three examples of their behaviour as they ran from the rhinoceros which do not seem well-disciplined. [3 marks]

Exercise 6   The Storm

Read the passage and answer the combining question which follows.

Huge waves pounded the stone walls built to keep the sea at bay, smashing free huge blocks of marble and flinging them aside like pebbles, until the walls cracked and then collapsed.

> 1. 'Huge waves' pounded the sea walls. Explain fully the comparison used by the writer to show the strength of these waves. [2 marks]

Exercise 7   After the Storm

Read the passage and answer the combining question which follows.

Slowly at first, and then from every quarter, the flicker of tiny flames was seen as Venetians went round their stricken city by candlelight. When they met they all said the same thing: that if the wind had not dropped, and if a third high tide had entered the lake to boost the two already there, then quite likely Venice would not have survived.

Because of the gradual melting of the ice at the North Pole, the level of the sea has been rising, threatening to reach the level of the streets in the city. At the same time the area around the river has been sinking, taking the city with it. Some of this sinking is natural and inevitable, but it has been accelerated by the extraction of fresh water from the ground beneath the city for use in huge industrial developments.

> i. The level of the sea has been 'threatening to reach the level of the streets in the city'. Give one natural and one man-made cause of this threat. [2 marks]

Exercise 8 Protection of the Environment

Read the passage and answer the combining question which follows.

It has now become abundantly clear that, if schemes for the protection of the environment are not initiated and controlled by local people, they stand little chance of success. It is vitally important to ensure that the wealth of expertise that still remains in living memory is not lost.

> What will be the two results, according to the writer, 'if schemes for the protection of the environment are not initiated and controlled by local people'? [2 marks]

Exercise 9 Coral Animals

Read the passage and answer the combining question which follows.

Coral animals, the remarkable little creatures that build coral reefs, are responsible for creating the largest structures made by life on earth, big enough, in some cases, to dwarf even the most ambitious buildings constructed by humankind.

> i. Explain fully why the writer describes coral animals as 'remarkable'. [2 marks]

Exercise 10 Emma

Read the passage and answer the combining question which follows.

Emma leant back against the seat of the train carriage, her eyes closed, trying to get her breathing back to normal. What a start to the day! Her mother had phoned as she was trying to gulp down some breakfast, with a reminder that it was her father's birthday the following week. Emma was irritated that her mother could not have picked a more convenient time to phone and, in any case, she had never forgotten her father's birthday before. The drive to the station, which should have taken ten minutes, took longer because of the accident on the motorway.

> i. Give two reasons why Emma was late for the train. [2 marks]
>
> ii. Give two reasons why Emma was annoyed at her mother. [2 marks]

Chapter **20**

More exercises in combining questions

Exercise 1 The Great Wall of China

Read the passage and answer the combining questions which follow.

Nomadic tribes would harass and plunder agricultural areas, making farming impossible unless some ways were found to stop them. The farmers attacked them to try to force them away. Although it was expensive, they tried to bring about peaceful relations with them, but this tactic was a blow to their pride and consequently short-lived. Finally, they built barriers to prevent invasion and to allow for military defence. Through time, the building of walls was the solution most consistently relied upon. These walls were eventually linked up to form what came to be known as the Great Wall.

In the construction of the Great Wall, the recruitment of labour was a major difficulty. In the early stages, soldiers were used to do this work, and sometimes local peasants as well as the army were forced to take part. During the reign of one emperor, over a million men were engaged in the construction of the Wall. A special penalty existed during the reign of other emperors, under which convicted criminals were made to work on the Wall as a way of atoning for their crimes.

i. The farmers 'tried to bring about peaceful relations' with the nomadic tribes. Apart from this, what other two methods did they use to deal with them?   [2]

ii. What three types of labourers built the Great Wall? Use no more than twelve words in your answer.   [3]

[Total: 5 marks]

Exercise 2 Building the Great Wall

Read the passage and answer the combining questions which follow.

Building materials could be passed from hand to hand in a human chain, which spared the builders the trouble of long walks on narrow mountain trails, thus avoiding collision. Simple tools, like the handcart and rope levers, were also used, and sure-footed animals such as goats and donkeys could be driven up the mountain carrying bricks. Donkeys were made to carry baskets filled with bricks on their backs; as for the goats, bricks were tied on to their horns.

i.   If it had not been possible to pass building materials from hand to hand, what two problems would the builders have had?   [2]

ii. Explain fully what use was made of donkeys in the building work.   [2]

[Total: 4 marks]

Exercise 3 The Lone Walker

Read the passage and answer the combining questions which follow.

As the door closes behind him and he steps away from the house, he feels a clarifying pleasure in the cold night air and, he can admit it, in being briefly alone. If only the hospital where he worked were further away. Irresponsibly, he prolongs his walk by half a minute by going across the square, rather than down Warren Street. The few fine snowflakes he saw earlier have vanished, and during the evening it has rained; the square's paving stones and cobbled gutters shine cleanly in the white street light. The square is deserted, which also pleases him.

i.   Give three reasons why the character is enjoying being outside.   [3]

ii. Explain fully what the weather has been like before the character goes out.   [2]

[Total: 5 marks]

Exercise 4 A Thistle Year

Read the passage and answer combining questions which follow.

To the cowboy who lives half his day on his horse and loved his freedom as much as a wild bird, a 'thistle year' (a season in which thistles grew particularly well) was a hateful period of restraint. His small, low-roofed mud house was then like a prison to him, for the tall thistles hemmed it in and shut out the view on all sides. On his horse he was compelled to keep to the narrow cattle tracks and to draw in or draw up his legs to keep them from the long, prickling spines. In those distant, primitive days the cowboy, if he was a poor man, wore nothing on his feet but a pair of iron spurs.

The thistles when dead were just as great a nuisance as the living thistles. In their dead, dry condition, they would sometimes stand all through December and January when the days were hottest and the threat of fire was ever present in all our minds.

i. Explain fully why, for the cowboy, a thistle year was 'a hateful period of restraint'. [2]

ii. Give two reasons why the cowboy was 'compelled' to keep to the narrow cattle tracks. [2]

iii. Explain fully why there was a particularly serious threat of fire during December and January. [2]

[*Total: 6 marks*]

Exercise 5 The Destroyed Novel

Read the passage and answer the combining questions which follow.

Having spent some time working, I had just written and counted my first five hundred words when I remembered baby Octavia; I could hear her making small, happy noises somewhere along the corridor, but felt it time I should go and see if she was doing something destructive, like unravelling the end of the hall carpet. She was remarkably persistent in destruction for her age.

I was rather dismayed when I realised she was in Lydia's room and that I must have left the door open, for Lydia's room was always full of nasty objects like aspirins {pain killers] and bottles of ink: I rushed along to rescue her and the sight that met my eyes when I opened the door was enough to make anyone quake. She had her back to the door and was sitting in the middle of the floor surrounded by a sea of torn, strewed, chewed paper. I stood there transfixed, watching the neat small back of her head and her thin, stalk-like neck and flowering curls; suddenly she gave a great screech of delight and ripped another sheet of paper. 'Octavia,' I said in horror, and she started guiltily, and looked round at me with a charming and deprecating smile; her mouth, I could see, was wedged full of wads of Lydia's new novel.

Source: *The Millstone* by Margaret Drabble, Penguin Books

i.   Give three reasons why the writer feels she should check up on the baby. [3]

ii. Give two reasons why the writer was upset when she realised where the baby was. [2]

iii. Explain fully what the baby had been doing. [3]

[*Total: 8 marks*]

Exercise 6 Benjamin

Read the passage and answer the combining questions which follow.

'Bye, Mum!' shouted Benjamin as he rushed to get the school bus. He was looking forward to his day; a double lesson of his favourite subject. If anyone had asked him for the reason for this devouring interest, he would have said he didn't really know. However, his passion for literature had begun when his grandfather, himself a keen reader, had given him a copy of a famous novel when he was only eleven years old; he had found the story so fascinating that he had finished reading it within the week. His grandfather's favourite subject at school had been literature and, like him, he had read this novel over and over again. In Benjamin's school, there was a limited number of spaces for the literature class, and Benjamin was more than a little anxious he might not be accepted. When one of the teachers of the subject retired at the start of the holidays, that had made him even more anxious. However, he was one of the lucky few, and loved every minute of the classes. He acted out – in his head at least – the key events in the novels he read, and pretended – again in his head – to be the central character. As he sat on the school bus, Benjamin thought of the notebook hidden in his cupboard, where he had begun to write his own novel, in order to be famous himself one day.

i.   Give three reasons why it was appropriate that Benjamin's grandfather gave him a copy of a famous novel. [3]

ii. Explain fully how we can tell that Benjamin found the novel his grandfather gave him 'fascinating'. [2]

iii. Give two reasons why Benjamin was anxious that he might not be accepted for the literature class. [2]

iv. How can we tell that Benjamin 'loved every minute of the classes'? Give two reasons for your answer. [2]

v.   Explain fully the purpose of Benjamin's notebook. [2]

[*Total: 11 marks*]

Chapter **21**

Appreciating the ways writers make use of language

At the beginning of Chapter 13 we considered a number of questions which you might ask yourself before answering a question in a comprehension examination. The final two questions in the list were:

- is the question asking only about the story or argument of the text?
- is the question asking only about particular features of language e.g. figures of speech?

The answer to these two questions is dealt with in Assessment Objective (vi) for O Level English Language. This Assessment Objective tests the extent to which you are able to appreciate the way writers make use of language. You will almost certainly be asked a question in the examination which you take that will be testing your ability to respond to the skill of the writer of the comprehension passage you are reading.

Questions about the writer's craft go beyond literal and inferential comprehension. They assume that the reader understands the meaning of what has been written, but draw the reader into responding to writing skills which are the signs of a good piece of writing. The answers to literal and inferential questions really answer the question 'What?' or 'Who?', whereas answers to questions about the writer's craft really answer the question 'How?'

Example 1   The Accident

The police car sirens sounded; people stood aside and cars stopped to let them past. It was clear that an emergency had occurred up ahead. Ambulances sped along the road and screeched to a halt at the spot where the collision had taken place. As the ambulance crew stepped out of the vehicle to examine the injured drivers, it seemed that a real-life drama was about to begin.

Question : Why does the writer say that the ambulances 'sped' along the road? [1]

Answer 1 The writer says that the ambulances sped along the road because they were going to the scene of an accident.

Answer 2 The writer says that the ambulances sped along the road because he wants to emphasise that they were going very fast.

Answer 3 The ambulances sped along the road because the drivers were racing one another.

Exercise 1

Working with a partner, decide which mark should be allocated to each answer, giving reasons for the mark you have decided. You should have something like this:

Answer 1 scores 0 mark. It is true that the ambulances were going to the scene of the accident, but that is not what the question is asking. This answer is an answer to a different question, such as 'Where were the ambulances going?' This particular question is drawing your attention to the use of the word 'sped'.

Answer 2 scores 1 mark, because it does, in fact, answer the question by focusing on the word 'sped'. This answer appreciates that the writer could have used, for example, the words 'went' or 'drove' or 'travelled'. The meaning would not have been affected in that we would still have known that what is being described is the scene of an accident and the ambulances going there to help the injured. But the word 'sped' has been carefully chosen by the writer to give the impression of a great dash, of the greatest possible speed, because this is a serious emergency.

Answer 3 scores 0 marks because, although it recognises the fact that the word' sped' has connotations of speed, it makes the wrong connection, and the wrong inference that the drivers were speeding because they were in some sort of competition with one another.

Example 2   Visiting Easter Island

Easter Island is the most remote inhabited place in the entire world. Until an airport was made in the 1960s, it was all but impossible to get to, because the only connection with the rest of the world was a ship which visited the island once a year. There is now something called a hotel on the island, so at least now visitors can stay there.

> **Question**: 'There is now something called a hotel on the island'. Why does the writer not simply say 'There is a hotel on the island'? *[1 mark]*

Answer 1: The writer thinks the reader might not know what a hotel is and so he gives an explanation.

Answer 2: The writer wants to emphasise that visitors can stay on the island whereas in the past this wasn't possible.

Answer 3: The writer wants to tell us that by our own standards it is a very basic hotel. It would hardly be described as a hotel by most people.

Exercise 2

Working with a partner, decide which mark should be allocated to each answer, giving reasons for the mark you have decided. You should have something like this.

Answer 1 scores 0 mark because it is not reasonable to assume that someone capable of understanding a passage at this level would not know the meaning of a common and international word like 'hotel'.

Answer 2 scores 0 mark because it is a literal comprehension of the question, explaining only the advantage of now having a hotel on the island. However, it does not answer the question, which was asking for an explanation of why the writer says 'there is something called a hotel' and not 'there is a hotel'. This answer merely answers the first possible question, i.e. 'why does the writer tell us there is now a hotel?' rather than the real question ,which is 'why does the writer tell us there is something called a hotel?'

Answer 3 scores 1 mark because it responds to the key difference between the obvious question of why the writer tells us there is a hotel and the more subtle question of why the writer tells us there is something of a hotel. The word 'something' is used unusually and this answer focuses on that. There is a clear difference between a 'hotel' and 'something of a hotel', and the thrust of the use of the word 'something' is that it isn't much of a hotel, it's of poor standard, it isn't what we would expect a hotel to be.

Example 3   The Streets of Dhaka

As Hemu walked through the streets of Dhaka, he marvelled at the vastness of the city, so different from the little village he had left behind. He loved the feel of the city, the crowds making their way though the evening darkness, the roar of the traffic and the illuminated buildings like stars by which people navigated their way home.

Question: Explain fully why the writer says that the buildings were 'like stars'? [2 marks]

Answer 1: The writer says that the buildings were like stars because they were lit up.

Answer 2: The writer says that the buildings were like stars because they were beautiful.

Answer 3: The writer says that the buildings were like stars because they were bright and people used them to work out their whereabouts.

Exercise 3

Working with a partner, decide which mark should be allocated to each answer, giving reasons for the mark you have decided. You should have something like this.

Answer 1: score 1 mark because it makes one comparison between stars and the buildings. The building were bright and twinkling with light, just as the stars in the sky are bright and twinkling. However, if the mark allocation had been taken into consideration, and the word 'fully' in the question, it should have been seen that there are two parts to the answer.

Answer 2: scores 0 marks because, although most people would consider the stars to be beautiful, there is nothing in the passage to link stars to beauty. The answer is not based on the passage but rather comes from the opinion of the person answering the question.

Answer 3: scores 2 marks because it has responded both to the allocation of two marks for the question and to the presence of the word 'fully' in the question. It focuses on the word 'illuminated' in the text and made that link between the brightness of the stars and the lights in the buildings. It has then gone on to focus on the word 'navigated' and make the further connection that sailors use the stars to navigate their way through the sea, in the same way as people in the city use the light from buildings to find their way through the city.

Exercise 4   The Flood

Read the passage and answer the writer's craft questions which follow.

People came down from the safety of the upper floors of their houses to inspect the ruin caused by the flood: oil stains, debris, filth and drowned animals were everywhere. Slowly at first, and then from every part of the city, the flicker of tiny flames was seen as the people went round their stricken city by candlelight. The candle flames danced in the soft breeze and their gentle movements seemed to mock the occasion.

> i.   People 'went round their stricken city'. What effect is gained by the word 'stricken' that would not have been achieved by the word 'flooded'? [1]
>
> ii. Why is it appropriate to say that the candle flames 'danced'? [1]
>
> iii. Explain fully why the writer means when he tells us that the candle flames 'seemed to mock the occasion'? [2]
>
> [*Total: 4 marks*]

Exercise 5   The Kitchen Table

Read the passage and answer the writer's craft questions which follow.

We sat down to table in the cramped kitchen. The table was left from the shop's bakery days, a massive piece of rough-cut pine cross-hatched with knife scars into which veins of ancient dough, dried to the consistency of cement, had worked to produce a smooth marbly finish.

Source: *Chocolat* by Joanne Harris, Black Swan

> i. What effect is produced by the writer's use of 'scars' instead of, for example, 'marks'? [1]
>
> ii. The marks on the kitchen table have 'veins of ancient dough'. Explain exactly what is being described here. [2]
>
> iii. Why does the writer describe the surface of the table in places as 'marbly'? [1]
>
> [*Total: 4 marks*]

Exercise 6   The Market in Mumbai

Read the passage and answer the writer's craft questions which follow.

Rohit meandered through the market in Mumbai. He was on holiday after all, and the day was stretched out before him like a century.

> i. Explain fully what effect the writer gains by her use of the word 'meandered'. [2]
>
> ii. Rohit was on holiday for the day. Why, therefore, does the writer compare the day to a century? [1]
>
> [*Total: 3 marks*]

Exercise 7   Spring

Read the passage and answer the writer's craft questions which follow.

Spring has come with little prelude, like turning a rocky corner into a sheltered valley, and gardens and their borders have blossomed suddenly, lush with daffodils, irises, tulips. Even the derelict houses of Les Maurads are touched with colour, but here the ordered gardens have run to rampant eccentricity: a roof carpeted with dandelions; violets poking out of a crumbling facade.

Source: *Chocolat* by Joanne Harris, Black Swan

> i. Explain fully why the writer describes the arrival of spring as 'like turning a rocky corner into a sheltered valley.' [2]
>
> ii. What effect does the word 'lush' have on our picture of spring? [1]
>
> iii. What does the writer mean when she describes the roof as being 'carpeted' with dandelions? [1]
>
> [*Total: 4 marks*]

Exercise 8   The New School

Read the passage and answer the writer's craft questions which follow.

Padma and Rita approached the gates of their new school with some dread and trepidation. Girls in uniforms identical to theirs snaked in front of them; Padma and Rita envied their assurance, their composure – this was familiar territory to them, whereas Padma and Rita were explorers in new territory.

'There are millions of them!' whispered Rita. 'Absolutely millions!'

i. Explain fully what effect is achieved by the word 'snaked'?	[2]
ii. In what way were Padma and Rita 'explorers in new territory'?	[2]
iii. There could not have been 'millions' of girls in the school. Why, then does the writer have Rita say that there were?	[1]

[Total: 5 marks]

Chapter **22**

More exercises in appreciating writers' craft

Exercise 1 The Gardener

Read the passage and answer the writer's craft questions which follow.

There is a look of desperation about him nowadays as he works, digging and hoeing furiously – sometimes bringing out great clumps of shrubs and flowers along with the weeds – the sweat running down his back. He does not enjoy the exercise. I see his face as he works, features crunching with the effort. He seems to hate the soil he digs, to hate the plants with which he struggles. He looks like a miser forced to shovel banknotes into a furnace: hunger, disgust and reluctant fascination. And yet he never gives up. Watching him I feel a familiar pang of fear, though for what I am not sure. He is like a machine this man, my enemy.

Source : *Chocolat* by Joanne Harris, Black Swan

---

  i. Why does the writer describe the man's face as 'crunching with effort'? [1]

 ii. The writer describes the man as being 'like a miser, forced to shovel banknotes into a furnace'. Explain fully what the writer is saying here. [2]

iii. When the writer says that the man was 'like a miser' she is using a simile. Pick out and write down another simile from the passage and explain why it is effective. [3]

  [*Total: 6 marks*]

Exercise 2 The Well Dressed Lady

Read the passage and answer the writer's craft questions which follow.

'Well, if it's no trouble...' Her manner was different today. There was a kind of crispness in her voice, a studied casualness which masked a high level of tension. She was wearing a black straw hat trimmed with a ribbon and a coat – also black – which looked new.

'You're very chic today,' I observed.

She gave a sharp crack of laughter. 'No-one's said that to me for a while, I'll tell you,' she said.

Source : *Chocolat* by Joanne Harris, Black Swan

i. Explain fully what the writer means by describing the woman's behaviour as 'studied casualness'. [2]

ii. The woman gave 'a sharp crack of laughter'. Explain fully what effect is achieved here that would not be achieved merely by 'she laughed' [2]

[*Total: 4 marks*]

Exercise 3 The Mountain Journey

Read the passage and answer the writer's craft questions which follow.

There was a track, but it kept on dividing. Part of my mind had to keep concentrating on which path to follow, the other part wandered in a way that had not been possible for some time. It felt like an animal which had been tethered for a long time and had now been released. At long last the labours and mental stress of the last three months were behind me. Now that there was no need to plan, discuss, argue or talk, my step lightened and began to quicken as I journeyed on through this silent place.

i. Explain fully why part of the writer's mind 'felt like an animal which had been tethered'. [2]

ii. The writer says 'my step lightened and began to quicken'. Apart from the notion of speed, what other idea is the writer suggesting here? [1]

[*Total: 3 marks*]

Exercise 4 The Traveller

Read the passage and answer the writer's craft questions which follow.

Jungle once more shrouded the path I was following. I plunged into the undergrowth, grateful that the path was still visible, but instead of simply having to put one foot in front of the other in order to go forward, I had to keep on climbing.

i. What effect is achieved by the writer's use of the word 'shrouded' that would not have been achieved by the word 'hid'? [1]

ii. The writer says 'instead of simply having to put one foot in front of the other'. What does his use of this expression tell you about the nature of his progress so far? [1]

[Total: 2 marks]

Exercise 5   Cell Phones

For many people, cell phones are a lifeline, a connection to family and friends, a way of keeping in touch with the work place in a fast moving world where we never seem to have enough time to complete all the jobs we have planned. They provide an oasis of calm into which we can step from the desert of modern living. But for others, cell phones are the scourge of modern society. You only have to watch people who are, supposedly, on an afternoon in each other's company. What are they doing? They are engrossed in conversation with someone other than their companion, their cell phone pressed to their ear as if their life depended on this little rectangular jewel.

i. Why does the writer describe the cell phone as a 'lifeline'? [1]

ii. Explain fully what the writer means when she says that cell phones 'provide an oasis of calm'. [2]

iii. Pick out and write down the single word in the passage which links to this idea of 'oasis'. [1]

iv. Why does the writer describe cell phones as sometimes being a 'scourge'? [1]

v. Explain fully what is meant by 'this little rectangular jewel'. [2]

[Total: 7 marks]

Exercise 6   Nizam and Hemu

It was easy to see that Nizam and Hemu were excellent English teachers. Their students were clay in their hands, as they moulded them through gentle correction of their grammatical errors and the praising of their achievements.

They loved English literature and lit a flame in many of their students which would never be extinguished. When the bell rang to signal the end of one lesson and the beginning of the next, their students flew down the corridor to their classrooms. They were obviously passionate about teaching and this showed in the excellent results they achieved and the high regard in which they were clearly held by the Principal of the school as well as by their students.

i. Explain fully why the writer describes the students of Nizam and Hemu as 'clay in their hands'. [2]

ii. Pick out and write down the single word in the passage which adds to the idea of 'clay'. [1]

iii. What is the 'flame' referred to by the writer? [1]

iv. What effect is produced by the use of the word 'flew' which would not be produced by 'went'? [1]

[Total: 5 marks]

Chapter **23**

Quotation questions and vocabulary questions

Assessment Objective (vi), as we have already seen, tests your ability to appreciate the ways in which writers make use of language, while Assessment Objective (v) tests your ability to evaluate information. You have examined different types of questions which test these abilities and completed exercises to improve your skills.

Another type of question which tests your ability both to appreciate ways in which writers make use of language and to evaluate information is the quotation question. In a quotation question, you are asked to find a word or expression in the text which means the same as another word or expression which comes either from the text also or which is a synonym provided by the writer of the question.

Example 1

Read the short passage and answer the question which follows.

The Beauty of Animals

Whenever we see pictures of animals or look at them in a zoo, we are often amazed by their beauty. The tiger, with black and yellow stripes, is a truly magnificent creature, while the leopard is equally eye-catching, with its richly spotted fur.

> **Question:** Write down one word which emphasises the writer's admiration of animals' beauty.

The key word in the question is the word 'admiration', which means wonder and delight. We must therefore scrutinise the text carefully to find a link with wonder and delight, linked to 'beauty', another important word in the question. Reading the text with 'wonder' and 'beauty' at the front of our minds enables us to home in on 'amazed' and 'magnificent' and 'eye-catching'. Any one of these words, in fact, is sufficient to answer the question.

Another important factor in giving a correct answer here is to examine the rubric carefully for what we are being asked to give as an answer. In this particular question, the rubric asks for one word. Consequently, the answers 'amazed by their beauty' or 'equally eye-catching' are incorrect, because they infringe the rubric, as Examiners say, that is they do not give the answer asked for. It is a pity that such answers would fail to score the available mark in the examination when there is clearly understanding behind them.

Exercise 1   The Rain Forests

Read the short passage and answer the question which follow.

Scientists, now keenly aware of dangers to the earth's environment, see the destruction of the rain forests as a major peril for Brazil and also for the rest of the world. Politicians have joined scientists to try to stop the foolish waste of the precious resources of these forests.

i. What two consecutive words in the passage tell us that scientists are not lacking in knowledge about what is happening to the rain forests. [1]

ii. Pick out and write down the single word in the passage which tells us that the writer thinks that the destruction of the rain forests is silly. [1]

[*Total: 2 marks*]

Exercise 2   Climate Change

Read the short passage and answer the question which follow.

Even more alarming is the threat to the world's climate. The burning of the trees accelerates the warming up of the earth's atmosphere, which scientists say will bring dramatic changes to our climate. Moreover, the blazing torches of the jungle will add to the harmful gases that cars and modern industries are pouring into the air we breathe.

i. What single word in the passage tells us that the earth's atmosphere is getting warmer and warmer? [1]

ii. Pick out and write down an expression from the passage which tells us that the burning forests are both bright and hot. [2]

[*Total: 3 marks*]

Exercise 3 Amy

Read the short passage and answer the questions which follow.

The next moment, though, she saw something more reassuring. In the far corner of the cave a large white cloth screen was being erected, musicians were gathering and people were taking their places for some sort of show. An old man made his entrance by the side of the screen, dressed in a tattered, grimy cloak. But it was his intense expression that startled Amy. Her feelings of uneasiness returned as she watched him gaze round the audience.

i. Amy saw something 'reassuring'. What single word used later in the passage shows that later she was no longer feeling reassured? [1]

ii. Pick out and write down the single word which shows that the old man's clothes were dirty. [1]

[*Total: 2 marks*]

Exercise 4 After the Show

Read the short passage and answer the questions which follow.

The audience broke into a stuttering applause, clearly moved by the realism of the contest. The old man appeared by the side of the screen, holding up the two puppets, the fighters in the grim contest. One of the puppets bore a fearful resemblance to the old man's assistant, the little boy with his large, sad eyes. Amy panicked wildly. She ran outside, stumbling down the steps, blundering past the crowd, desperate to get away from the ghastly presence in the cave.

i. Write down one word which shows us that the audience did not start to clap at once after the show. [1]

ii. Amy 'ran outside'. Write down two separate words which show that she was frightened as she ran. [2]

[*Total: 3 marks*]

Another type of question which tests your ability to evaluate the language used by writers is the vocabulary question. In the 'O' level examination, the question immediately before the summary question offers you eight single words or phrases and asks you to explain what five of these mean as they are used in the passage.

This question is designed to test your understanding only. Consequently, you will not be penalised for misspelling or grammatical inaccuracy. This means that if you offer a noun as a synonym for an verb, there will be no penalty, provided that understanding is demonstrated in your answer.

Exercise 5   Keeping Pets

Read the passage, the question and the sample answers which follow.

It is a curious thing, but when you keep animals as pets you imagine they will behave exactly as you would like them to.

Question: For the word 'curious', give one word or short phrase (of not more than seven words) which has the same meaning that the word has in the passage.

Answer 1: Curious means wanting to know.

Answer 2: Curious means strangeness.

Answer 3: Curious means strange.

Answer 4: Curious means strainge.

Answer 5: Curious mean strange and wanting to know.

Answer 6: Curious – strange or wanting to know.

Answer 7: Curious – wanting to know or strange.

Working with a partner, work out which of these seven answers would get one mark and which would get no mark. You should have something like this:

Answer 1 scores no mark. This is because, although 'wanting to know' can be an acceptable synonym for 'curious', it does not fit the context. The rubric specifically asks for the meaning of the word in the passage, and it is not 'wanting to know'.

Answer 2 scores 1 mark. This is because, although it gives a noun as a synonym for an adjective, it shows understanding of the word 'curious' in the context. There is no penalty for incorrect grammatical form.

Answer 3 scores 1 mark. This is a correct synonym for 'curious' as it is used in the passage. Answering in the correct grammatical form is good, but scores no more than an answer which does not so do. It is understanding, not grammar, which is being tested here.

Answer 4 scores 1 mark. This is a correct synonym for 'curious' as it is used in the passage. The spelling is incorrect, but that does not matter here. It is understanding, not spelling, which is being tested.

Answer 5 scores 0 mark. This is because, although 'strange' is correct, it is spoiled by the addition of the wrong answer 'wanting to know'. The word 'and' in the answer indicates that this is one answer, in which two words are joined to form one answer, using the word 'and'.

Answer 6 scores 1 mark. The use of the word 'or' indicates a second attempt, and only the first answer is examined. So this answer scores 1 mark for the first answer, which is correct, and the second answer, which happens to be incorrect, is ignored.

Answer 7 scores 0 mark. The use of the word 'or' indicates a second attempt, and only the first answer is examined. So this answer scores 0 mark for the first answer, which is incorrect, and the second answer, which happens to be correct, is ignored.

Exercise 6   Benjamin

In the short passage which follows, for each of the words 'occasionally' and 'declined', give one word or short phrase (of not more than seven words) which has the same meaning that the word has in the passage.

It was hardly surprising that Benjamin did so well in the examination, as he did four, and occasionally five, hours homework every night. He studied at weekends and was a delight to his teachers because he never declined to take on extra homework tasks.   [2 *marks*]

Exercise 7   Sophie

In the short passage which follows, for each of the words 'teeming', 'apprehensive' and 'thrilling', give one word or short phrase (of not more than seven words) which has the same meaning that the word has in the passage.

Sophie stood on the edge of the pavement waiting for the traffic lights to change, so that she could cross the road. The city was teeming with people, some in cars, some, like her, on foot. She had been apprehensive about coming to Chittagong, but, now that she was here, she found it a thrilling place to live.

[*3 marks*]

Exercise 8   Keeping Pavlo Warm

In the short passage which follows, for each of the words 'imitate', 'crack', and 'alternative', give one word or short phrase (of not more than seven words) which has the same meaning that the word has in the passage.

We turned up the heating in the house to its highest temperature, trying to imitate the jungles of South America. We gave Pavlo a drawer to be his warm bed. We had to push the drawer closed for extra warmth, except for a crack to allow for air. Every morning he awoke early and found that his hot water bottle had gone cold. So he went looking for alternative warmth.

[3 marks]

Exercise 9   World Food Shortage

In the short passage which follows, for each of the words 'astonishing', 'shortage', 'consequence' and 'explosion', give one word or short phrase (of not more than seven words) which has the same meaning that the word has in the passage.

The world's population is increasing at an astonishing rate and in some countries there is a shortage of food, although this is often caused by natural disasters rather than as a direct consequence of the population explosion.

[4 marks]

Chapter

Combining information in the summary question

We know that Assessment Objective v in 'O' Level English is to select, retrieve, evaluate and combine information from written texts, and we have looked at what these skills mean as far as answering one, two or even three mark questions on a given text is concerned. However, there is another type of question which tests your ability to select, retrieve, evaluate and combine information, and that is the summary question. In any summary question, you are asked to read a passage and show that you have understood it by writing a short text of your own based on the original. The subject matter of your short text, or summary, will depend on what you have been asked to do.

What follows is a list of typical summary tasks. What you are asked to do here (or indeed in any examination) is called the 'rubric'.

i.   Write a summary of the problems encountered on the journey.

ii. Summarise the skills the writer thinks are necessary to become a good swimmer.

iii. Write a summary of the steps taken by the main character to trace her missing friend.

iv. Write a summary of what the men and their leader did when they first set out, what they did when they were confronted by the rhinoceros, and how the author reacted to its presence.

v.   Summarise the ways in which coral reefs are under threat.

The first stage is to read the rubric properly and be quite clear in your mind what you are being asked to do.

The second stage is to carefully read the passage, or the area of the passage which you are being asked to summarise, at least twice. If you have answered comprehension questions before arriving at the summary question (and in your 'O' Level examination that will be the case), you will already have done a lot of reading of the passage anyway, but it is still a good idea to read it again with the summary rubric in mind.

The third stage is to select the content points. These are the pieces of information which you need to follow the rubric. So in the first summary task, the content points will be problems encountered, in the second task the content points will be skills necessary to become a good swimmer, and so on.

Exercise 1 The Uses of Silk

Read the passage and answer the question which follows it.

At first, silk was the monopoly of the Chinese Imperial family, who used it for sunshades and banners. As it became more plentiful, it was utilised for clothing, but exclusively for members of the court. Only the Emperor and his first wife wore yellow silk – the colour of the sun. His other wives wore violet, as did high-ranking officers. Those of the second rank wore red and the rest had black. Later, the favour of being able to wear silk was extended to landowners and merchants who sought to out-dazzle each other in a riot of colour. Eventually, ordinary people could wear silk clothes, although they were not so elaborately embroidered, nor did they have the tea-cups of lacquered silk, customary with the wealthy. Silk achieved importance in other ways. Until the invention of paper, people wrote on it. It became a popular currency, with even taxes paid in it.

Question: Working with a partner, make a list of the six things people used silk for.

The first stage is to read the rubric carefully and be quite clear in your mind what you are being asked to do. In this case, the task is to list uses of silk. These words – used and silk – should be at the front of your mind as you approach stage two.

The second stage is to carefully read the passage at least twice. Remember to keep the key words – used and silk – at the front of your mind as you read.

The third stage is to select the content points. These are the pieces of information which you need to follow the rubric. The word 'used' appears in the first sentence and it is easy to link it to 'sunshades' and 'banners', which follow closely after the word 'used'. The word 'utilised' appears in the second sentence, and 'utilised' is a synonym for 'used'. Good writers avoid repeating words and so this writer has used a synonym, but because we have the rubric key words—used and silk – at the front of our minds, we do not miss the signpost. So it is clear that silk was utilised, or used, for clothing.

The third, fourth, fifth and sixth sentences, and the first part of the seventh, give details of the groups of people who were entitled to wear silk and the colours each group wore. These groups are the Emperor, his wives, high-ranking officers, landowner, merchants and ordinary people. However, because we have the key words at the front of our minds – silk and use – we are not tempted to use any of this material in our list of uses of silk, because this material gives extra information about the use of silk which we have already found, namely that it was used for clothing. But when we read on into the seventh sentence, with the key words – used and silk – at the front of our minds, we see that silk was used by wealthy people to make tea-cups.

The eighth sentence repeats the idea that silk was used and so, although no particular use is specified in the sentence, it is a further signpost and alerts us to the possibility that by reading on we will find other uses for silk. And so in the ninth sentence, we see that silk was used as writing material, and finally in the tenth sentence we see that silk was also used as money. The extra information about taxes is not a separate point, any more than the information given about the groups of people who wore silk and the colours that they wore. The information about taxes is linked to the idea of money, which we have already found as a point.

Answer

People used silk for:

   i. sunshades

  ii. banners

 iii. clothes

 iv. tea-cups

  v. paper

 vi. money

These six points are called the content points.

We saw that there are two sections of extra information in the passage. The first section is the detail about the people who were entitled to wear silk and the colours they wore. The second section of extra information is the reference to taxes. These sections of information are not content points because they are not particular uses of silk, which was the rubric. The purpose of these sections is to give additional information and colour to the passage , to elaborate on the basic information given about the uses people found for silk. They are called elaboration points.

Exercise 2   The Wearers of Silk

Question: Working with a partner, make a list of seven people or groups of people who wore silk, and write beside each group what colour of silk they wore. Do not include ordinary people in your list.

You should have something like this:

   i.   emperor – yellow

   ii. emperor's first wife – yellow

  iii. emperor's other wives – violet

  iv. high-ranking officers – violet

   v. second-ranking officers – red

  vi. other officers – black

 vii. landowners and merchants – many colours

In the exercise we have just done, we see that the section of the passage about people who wore silk and the colours they wore is not a section of elaboration. It is a section of content points because the rubric has changed.

Before looking for content points, it is important to be sure of the rubric and to isolate the key words and keep them at the front of your mind as you read the passage.

Exercise 3 A Bad Start

Read the passage and answer the question which follows it.

The day started off badly and got steadily worse and worse. My sister spent ages in the bathroom, even longer than usual, and so I was late with my shower.

When I was halfway to the bus stop, I realised I had left my bus pass on the kitchen table and had to go back for it, after which I raced back to the bus stop, sweating, dishevelled and breathless. My sister, of course, was already there, looking relaxed, demure and very well showered. She smiled a knowing smile at me as if to say 'Aren't brothers awful?' to her equally well groomed friends. To make matters worse, one of my sister's friends, Diana, was standing there with her; because I found Diana fascinating and pretty, and had been trying to pluck up the courage to speak to her for months, I felt awkward and embarrassed. Clearly, this was not the day for doing it; I quietly cursed myself for appearing so silly before her.

I dashed off the bus, glad to get away from my sister and Diana. As soon as I reached the class – it was science first period that day – I remembered that we had been given homework the last day. How could I have forgotten to do it? Groaning inwardly, I waited for the teacher to ask for the homework notebooks. I took a deep breath and put up my hand to confess.

'What do you mean, no homework?' hissed the teacher. 'It's lunchtime detention for you, and a letter home to your parents. I'm surprised at a boy like you forgetting your homework.'

My heart sank. My father would be furious with me.

Question: Working with a partner, make a list of the seven problems which the writer experienced that day. Use the three steps already outlined to complete this task.

You should have something like this:

  i. he was late having his shower

 ii. he left his bus pass on the table

iii. he was embarrassed to see Diana / behaved awkwardly with Padma

 iv. he had forgotten his science homework

  v. the teacher gave him lunchtime detention

 vi. the teacher was to going to send a letter to his parents

vii. his father would be angry with him

Exercise 4 Cafe India

Read the passage and answer the question which follows it.

Anu loved Cafe India and went there whenever she had a free afternoon. The coffee which was served there was perfect, the right blend of beans, not too strong, but with a full flavour. The service was excellent and she had come to know the waiters well, particularly the charming young man called Rajesh, a university student who worked part-time in Cafe India to pay for his studies. Sitting there today, Anu looked around the familiar space – with its checked table covers, cream walls, slightly fraying carpet – and thought that its familiarity was comforting. Sometimes, when it wasn't too hot, she liked to sit on the balcony, which gave a bird's eye view of the street below. She watched people chatting, young men watching girls passing by, and once she had witnessed a pickpocket in action, unaware that he was being watched from above. On other days, she met up with her friends, former teachers like herself, and they passed a happy time reminiscing about the good old days in the classroom. On other occasions, like today, she could read a book – crime novels were her favourites – and sip coffee contentedly as she pretended not to be listening in to other people's conversations, a secret delight.

> **Question**: Working with a partner, make a list of the seven things which Anu likes to do in Cafe India. Use the three steps already outlined to complete this task.

Exercise 5 Children in the Developing World

Read the passage and answer the question which follows it.

In the developing world, children actually create wealth. By the age of ten, perhaps, they are busy working on the family's land – harvesting the crops and herding cattle – or fishing. It is a sad fact that many children are also employed for long hours making carpets or doing other unskilled or repetitive tasks; but even the low wages they earn increase the family's earning power. Much younger children perform useful tasks like gathering sticks and dry wood to burn or fetching water from the nearest well or stream for washing and drinking. These children do not cost much to support for they sleep in the same room as their parents, need very little food and wear cast off clothing. Perhaps one or two brighter, or luckier, sons may be sent to school and, from the good city jobs their education procures them, they are able to send money back to the family. Also, in these societies where pensions or insurance or government welfare schemes are not usually available, children provide a source of help in times of periodic crisis like illness, drought, flood or famine.

> **Question**: Working with a partner, make a list of the seven ways in which children bring wealth to their families in developing countries. Use the three steps already outlined to complete this task.

Exercise 6   Children in the Developed World

Read the passage and answer the question which follows it.

One way to reduce the world's population is to persuade people to have fewer children. On the face of it, it is perhaps surprising that poor people want to have more children. In developed countries, children are a financial burden to their parents. More children mean a larger house and increased bills for food, food and clothing. The children are at school and college and usually cannot contribute to the family income significantly until they are old enough to leave the family and set up households of their own. Thus, the more children mother and father have to support, the more thinly will their income be stretched and the poorer they will be. The modern child often expects expensive toys, another restraint on the family budget, and expenses on school trips are another source of financial difficulty. Parents often feel that they cannot cope with many children. Besides, if both parents are working, there is no-one at home to take care of the younger children who are not at school, and childcare and nursery provision carry huge financial burdens.

> **Question**: Working with a partner, make a list of the six ways in which children in developed countries are a financial burden to their parents. Use the three steps already outlined to complete this task.

Exercise 7   A Frightening Experience

Read the passage and answer the question which follows it.

Salman was terrified. He had been on his way back home from his friend's house when the street lights had gone out and he was walking in pitch darkness. The wind had started howling, and Salman was reminded of a television programme he had watched recently in which wild dogs had attacked children for no apparent reason. They had come from nowhere, it seemed. Safe in the security of his warm home, Salman had dismissed the programme as foolish fantasy, but now he wasn't so sure. He realised that there was no-one about on the street, despite the fact that it was early evening. What if his watch had stopped, and it was much later than he thought? He would certainly be in for a row when he reached home. That thought did nothing to make him feel better. Suddenly he heard a snuffling sound. What was that? It got louder and louder. Then something wet brushed the back of his hand. He was petrified, his heart racing, his tongue sticking to the roof of his mouth. Was it a ghost creature? One of the wild dogs of the television programme?

Should he stand still or make a dash for his home, which was only a few yards away now? He peered into the darkness and, almost crying with relief, realised that the phantom was only the family pet dog, Rex. His imagination had been playing tricks on him.

> **Question**: Working with a partner, make a list of the seven things which happen to make Salman terrified. Use the three steps already outlined to complete this task.

Exercise 8 Anna

Read the passage and answer the question which follows it.

Malini drove along Ansari Road, concentrating on her driving, which was especially necessary at this time, the rush hour. However, she couldn't help thinking of her friend, Anna, and the news she had received that day that Anna's long term relationship with her boyfriend, Chris, had come to an end. Anna had put a brave face on as she told Malini about the fact that Chris had decided to go to Australia to study and that she wouldn't see him for at least three years. More than that, it seemed that his parents had never approved of Anna, something which clearly upset her and made her angry. Her own parents did little to make her feel better, she said, by complaining so much about Chris that she had started avoiding them, something she wasn't proud of, as they were getting older and needed her support more than she needed theirs.

Her father was to go into hospital soon for an operation, which was very much in her thoughts. As Malini climbed into her car to drive home, Anna smiled ruefully. 'And I failed my driving test last week,' she said.

> **Question**: Working with a partner, make a list of the seven things which are troubling Anna. Use the three steps already outlined to complete this task.

Chapter

More exercises in content summary points

Exercise 1 Queen

The passage which follows describes a journey the writer made with his elephant, Queen. With a partner, make a list of the problems the writer encountered with Queen during the journey. There is no need at this stage to write in paragraphs or to try to write in your own words. We will deal with that later. Concentrate in this exercise on content points.

As we were reaching the outskirts of the village, I saw a bus approaching us. Queen swerved abruptly, causing the collapse of a tea-stall. We came to a halt amongst a cascading river of cups and teapots. Glaring at us, his face a mottled purple, was the enraged owner.

'Er ... I'm frightfully sorry, sir,' I gasped. 'You see my ...'

'You! you!' the man shouted furiously. 'Everything gone, I'm ruined, I'll take you to court.'

'Now, sir,' Aditya said. 'There's no need for that. I am sure we can come to some financial agreement.' After the man had cooled down, we assessed the damage and compensation was paid. We couldn't get out of that village quickly enough; the drain on my nerves and on my pocket had been considerable. Besides, Queen unashamedly kept on helping herself to the cakes which were laid out on some market stalls.

Understandably her greed annoyed the owners and Salim would smack her trunk, whereupon she would squeeze her small brown eyes shut like a naughty little girl.

Eventually, we emerged into open countryside, and to our relief followed a track free of the din of traffic and the possibility of Queen's thieving. After a while we noticed that Queen was limping, a bad sign for our future progress, let alone Queen's comfort. Salim discovered the cause – a metal leg chain with small spikes had obviously been used on her by her previous owners. One of the spikes had caused an ulcer, but, Salim told me, hot-water and salt dressings applied nightly would cure it. Although his knowledge of elephant ailments reassured me, it took some time to make and apply these dressings.

Days passed and our journey continued. Queen plodded along,

her trunk plucking at branches from overhead trees, munching with contentment. Nevertheless, it was evident that her leg was still troubling her. Soon we came to another little town. The animal doctor there explained that Queen had a serious infection, and that she would need injections of antibiotics. Moreover, this difficult task was to be mine — and I was distinctly uneasy about it. After mentally marking a spot in Queen's enormous side, I shut my eyes and nervously plunged in the needle. I realised my attempt had failed when, with a squeal of rage, Queen trundled away with a broken needle wobbling precariously out of her side.

'That was incorrect,' the vet remarked needlessly. 'Place the needle in straight. Now, we will try again.'

You should have something like this:

i. Queen swerved to avoid a bus

ii. And knocked over a tea-stall

iii. The owner was angry

iv. And shouted at them

v. The writer had to pay compensation to the owner

vi. Queen helped herself to cakes from market stalls

vii. Which annoyed the stall owners

viii. Queen was limping

xi. Because a metal chain with spikes had been used on her leg

x. It took time to make and apply the dressings to Queen's leg

xi. We found out / the animal doctor told us that Queen had an infection

xii. She would need antibiotics

xiii. Which I would have to give her

xiv. I failed to give her the injection properly

Exercise 2 Octavia

In the passage which follows, a baby, Octavia, becomes ill and her mother is uncertain how to deal with this. With a partner, make a list of the reasons why the baby became ill, the symptoms of her illness and how her mother eventually decides to deal with the problem. There is no need at this stage to write in paragraphs or to try to write in your own words. We will deal with that later. Concentrate in this exercise on content points.

Autumn also brought other problems, such as the cold. I had never noticed the cold before, being healthy and energetic, but this year there was an unhealthily bitter October, with rain, fog, damp and frost at nights. I did not mind for myself, but I did not know how to keep the baby warm; when I put gloves on her, she chewed them, and then had to ride around in her pram with icy wet hands. She dribbled, too, and her chest was always damp. She resisted for some time, but in the end she caught a cold. At first it did not seem to worry her, but then she started to wake coughing in the night, and when she breathed she wheezed terribly like an old sheep. I did not know what to do with her, as I hated going to the doctor; I had thought to have finished with my dreary, time-wasting association with the Health Service at her birth, though I had already discovered that there was an unending succession of injections, inspections, vaccinations and immunisations yet to be endured. But up to this point, everything had been routine, and not a matter of choice. Now,

watching Octavia's nose run unbecomingly, and hearing her heavy spluttering, I knew I would have to decide to take her, and I found myself amazingly resistant to the idea. My reasons, I knew, were an inextricable mass of the childish and the selfishly diffident; I did not want to bother the doctor unnecessarily, having a great fear of bothering people, though perhaps more of a fear of being told that I am a nuisance, and I did not want to wait for two hours in a freezing cold waiting room with an active baby bouncing on my frail knee.

About twenty-four hours after I had made up my mind that I really ought to go, I consulted Lydia who was at first as perplexed by the problem as I was. She suggested that I should ring up the doctor and ask him to come and see me, instead of going to him; I had never even thought of doing this, which shows how little I had come to terms with the fact of my new life, and immediately thought how nice it would be if only I dare.

Source: *The Millstone* by Margaret Drabble, Penguin Books

Exercise 3 The Lonely Lighthouse

In the passage which follows, the crew of a delivery ship are approaching a lighthouse to deliver supplies to the three lighthouse keepers who live there. It is clear that something is wrong. With a partner, make a list of the problems which alerted the crew to the fact that something is wrong. There is no need at this stage to write in paragraphs or to try to write in your own words. We will deal with that later. Concentrate in this exercise on content points.

The delivery ship drew near the island and the crew noticed immediately that something was wrong. There was no welcoming flag flying from the lighthouse pole, although the delivery ship would have been expected. However, it was possible that the keepers were busy working out of sight on the other side of the island and, therefore, had not noticed the ship approaching. The captain ordered the ship's whistle to be sounded, but the shrill blast brought only thousands of sea-birds, from the cliff face, noisy and angry at being disturbed. There was no movement in or around the lighthouse. With mounting astonishment, the captain ordered a rocket to be fired over the island and, although it burst its colourful contents with a loud explosion, still nothing was seen of the keepers.

A small group of sailors was instructed to go ashore and find out what was wrong. Perhaps, they thought, the keepers were ill and could not venture out of the lighthouse. They climbed aboard a small boat and rowed ashore. The sailors' leader went to the top of the cliff on which the lighthouse perched, and began running along the pathway, calling out the names of the keepers.

But the only answer that came was the howling of the gales. The keepers normally opened the entrance gate of the yard when a delivery was expected, but on this particular day the gate was closed; it creaked open at his touch and he moved towards the lighthouse itself. He was surprised to find the front door was wide open and cautiously he entered. He continued to call out the names of the three men, but still no-one answered his shouts.

In the kitchen, two chairs stood next to the table, but the third chair had been knocked over and was lying on its side. Although it was freezing winter weather, the ashes in the fireplace were cold, showing that it was some time since a fire had been lit. All the pots and pans were clean and stacked neatly in their usual places. The clock on the shelf above the fireplace had stopped. The leader then went into the bedrooms and found that the beds were unmade, just as they would be if their occupants had just risen from them and left hurriedly. By now, he was finding it difficult to control his feelings. The hairs were standing up on the back of his neck, and he ran all the way back to the landing point. He breathlessly explained to the rest of the crew what he had found, andnormal practice was to complete the record daily. There was still no trace of the three keepers. It was becoming increasingly clear after this second search that no-one was there. two of the men volunteered

to go back with him to the lighthouse.

This group of three combed the outbuildings and the lighthouse itself. On reaching the top of the tower, they found that the warning lamp of the lighthouse was in working order, but there was a thin film of dust over it, suggesting that it had not been lit for some time. In addition, the last entry in the lighthouse's record book was for ten days earlier, although the normal practice was to complete the record daily. There was still no trace of the three keepers. It was becoming increasingly clear after this second search that no-one was there.

Exercise 4   School Uniform

The passage which follows describes the advantages and disadvantages of school uniform. With a partner, make a list of these advantages and disadvantages. There is no need at this stage to write in paragraphs or to try to write in your own words. We will deal with that later. Concentrate in this exercise on content points.

Many schools insist that the students wear school uniform. Probably the most popular type of school uniform is a shirt for both girls and boys, with black trousers and black skirt for male and female students respectively. A tie might also be worn. The heads of schools tend to favour the wearing of uniform for their students because it encourages a sense of belonging to the same group, like being in

one big family. Furthermore, school uniform puts an end to any possibility of some students being seen to be better off than others. If rich kids have more money to spend on designer clothes which are popular with the younger generation, the poorer kids know nothing about it. All students look the same, both rich and poor, and so school uniform is a great leveler of social groups. Children can concentrate on their studies without worrying whether or not they're dressed in the latest fashions. Fashion items can be kept in better condition because they are not being worn out in the rough and tumble of hectic school life. Students are able to concentrate on their studies better as there are no distractions of wondering who is the 'coolest' in the class and where everyone fits in the clothes competition.

Outside school, students are clearly identified. This is a good thing because they are ambassadors for their school and, if they misbehave outside school, the school is easily identified. A fear of bringing their school into disrepute, or a fear of being identified and their teachers or parents notified, might prevent some antisocial behaviour, especially in big cities. Conversely, good behaviour admired outside the school day could cause adults to see a particular school in a good light and want their children to attend it — well behaved students in uniform are an eloquent advertisement for their school. Very young children might aspire to be pupils at that school when they are older because the students inspire them by their exemplary behaviour.

On the other hand, some students are not so keen on wearing uniform, arguing that it suppresses their individuality and freedom to express themselves. What is the point, they say, in everyone being identically dressed? Doesn't that lead to robots rather than human beings, a bland group of people who are unable to think for themselves or to be creative? Others might say that parents have to buy yet more clothes for their children when they have to buy school shirts, trousers, ties, even special shoes, and so school uniform costs rather than saves money in the family, and puts an extra burden on the finances of a family. This is clearly more significant in a family with a limited income.

Exercise 5 Titanic

The passage which follows describes the events leading up to the sinking of the ship 'Titanic'. Working with a partner, make a list of the ways in which the actions of various people were responsible for the sinking. There is no need at this stage to write in paragraphs or to try to write in your own words. We will deal with that later. Concentrate in this exercise on content points.

Reports showed icebergs nearly in the path of the huge ship; unfortunately, not all these reports reached her control room. Nevertheless, the captain and his officers clearly knew there was a distinct possibility, even likelihood, of encountering an iceberg during the night. The captain must have known the risk he was taking in maintaining Titanic's speed, but decided to take it anyway; to have slowed his ship under the circumstances would have suggested a degree of timidity out of keeping with his character. Also his reputation was involved; he was understandably proud of it and did not want to damage it at this stage in his career. This marvellous vessel he commanded was on her first voyage while he, ironically, was on his last.

The lookouts were specifically warned to watch for icebergs, yet they did not seem particularly concerned about this possibility. Nor had any extra lookouts been posted. No special instructions were given to the ship's engineers to stand by for possible emergency manoeuvres. The advisability of slowing the vessel to allow more time to react should an iceberg be sighted ahead does not appear to have been considered by the captain. This is hardly surprising as it would have thwarted the hope for an even higher speed on the following day.

When further messages about icebergs came in from the ship Californian, the young radio operator on Titanic ignored them. Although he was dedicated to his profession, he did not have that degree of judgement which comes from years of experience. Besides, the glamour of his job had made him arrogant. Meanwhile, as one of the lookouts neared the end of his watch, an ominous smudge about the size of his hand loomed on the horizon dead ahead. The object grew rapidly in size and distinctness. Convinced that one of the icebergs he had been warned about was directly in Titanic's path, the lookout raised the alert and watched helplessly as the ship hurtled towards the sheer grey wall of ice.

Chapter (26)

Plan, organise, paragraph and punctuate in summary writing

Assessment Objective (viii) in 'O' Level English Language is to plan, organise and paragraph, using appropriate punctuation. These are all skills which are required in good summary writing. In this chapter we will look at ways in which these skills can be developed and improved.

Planning and organising your summary

You will have been given advice on planning and organising a piece of writing in the section of this book on Paper One. Planning and organising a summary is easier than planning and organising a piece of continuous writing, where you have only a topic to work on, and little or no guidance. Planning and organising a summary is more like planning and organising a piece of directed writing, in which the task is detailed for you. The way to plan and organise a summary is to follow the three stage system outlined in an earlier chapter.

The first stage is to read carefully the rubric, or the instructions given in the question itself. We have already dealt with the importance of sticking to the rubric by isolating the key words in it and keeping those in the front of your mind as you read the passage to be summarised.

The second stage is to read the passage at least twice. Of course, you will probably have already read the passage at least twice if you have answered comprehension questions before moving on to the summary question. Nevertheless, it is time well spent to read it again with the key words of the rubric at the front of your mind, because reading for the rubric of the summary is a different skill from reading the text to answer short factual, inferential or vocabulary questions.

The third stage in planning and organising your summary is to select the content points. So far, you have selected content points, you have written them down in a list. Now is the time to think about how to organise these content points so that the best possible summary can be produced with them. It is particularly important to have a system for planning and organising the summary points which will work for you in an examination when you are working against the clock.

You have a choice of two methods to use when it comes to this third stage of planning and organising your content points. It is a good idea to try the two ways and find the way which suits you. What is very important is that you have a system – the day of the examination is too late to experiment. Whatever method you use, you will be producing with it a first draft. Then you will be required to work on your first draft to produce a second draft. The third stage in planning and organising your material will result in your first draft.

The first method of planning and organising at this third stage, in other words to produce a first draft, is to do what you have already done in an earlier chapter, i.e. to make a list of content points. This method has the advantage of focusing your mind on the key words in the rubric. You approach the passage almost like target practice; you are encouraging yourself to get right to the heart of the text and the points made in it which relate to the question you have been given. The disadvantage of this method is that you have less of an idea how many words your final version will be. In an examination, you will have a word limit, and counting the words used in a first draft written in a list is of little help. However, many students find this a helpful way to plan and organise. It's a matter of choice, once you have tried both ways of planning and organising.

The second method of planning and organising at this third stage, in order to produce a first draft, is to write the content points down immediately into a paragraph. This method has the advantage of allowing you an accurate count at the end of your piece of writing; if you are in excess, you can start to delete words or sections of text, and if your word total is below the accepted number of words, you are free to search the passage for content points you may have overlooked. The disadvantage of this method is that it might be more difficult to get to the very heart of the content points in the passage, more difficult than in the 'target practice' method. Furthermore, if you copy down the words of the passage, you will stand less of a chance of scoring well when it comes to assessment of the use of own words; however, it is still possible to convert the original passage into your own words as you go along, or to work on re-casting it when you get to your second draft stage.

Exercise 1 Cycle Rickshaws in Dhaka

Read the passage which follows and answer the questions which follow.

So crowded are the city centre streets of Dhaka that sometimes the cycle rickshaw is the fastest means of transport. But cycle rickshaws can also be dangerous. Weaving in and out of traffic may save time but it is not always safe. Rickshaw cyclists sometimes try to shorten their journey times by going against the line of oncoming cars, and run the risk of being knocked off their cycles and seriously injured. Damage to cycle rickshaws has become quite commonplace too – it is easy to dent a tyre as you accidentally bump into the kerb in your attempt to dodge a wide vehicle like a bus or a car. Scraping the wheel of a cycle can also occur in this way, and it can be so expensive to have a cycle repaired that it causes financial hardship in many households. Cyclists would be safer if they wore helmets, but unfortunately they don't, as again this would put additional strain on the family budget. Passengers in cycle rickshaws would be safer if they were strapped in, but there are no safety belts installed in these colourful vehicles.

i. Make a list of the content points in the above passage.

ii. Summarise, in a single paragraph, the six ways in which rickshaw cyclists put themselves and other people in danger. Do not worry about the number of words used at this point as you are producing only a first draft.

iii. Which method of planning and organising content points did you feel more comfortable with?

Exercise 2 Tourists in Sri Lanka

Read the passage which follows and answer the questions which follow it.

Sri Lanka, which means 'Beautiful Lanka' is a favourite place for tourists. They enjoy its wonderful climate, its all-year round heat, especially those from colder, Western countries. They are drawn to the beauty of the island – the coastal regions and the mountainous areas – and it is hardly surprising that millions of visitors arrive each year to enjoy the delights of this country. Tourist hotels are of a high standard which is yet another attraction. They are well designed and modern, with facilities appreciated by their residents. The capital, Colombo, ensures an abundance of stores and boutiques to suit every taste and wallet, whether in the latest fashions, more traditional clothing, jewellery, perfumes ... the list is endless. Everyone can afford to shop in Colombo; there are many low budget shops and hawker stalls, as well as the glittering, glamorous stores. Tourists enjoy walking through neighbourhoods where traditional, local food is on sale in a variety of welcoming restaurants, where the very best and tastiest of food is sure to be served.

i.   Make a list of the content points in the above passage.

ii. Summarise, in a single paragraph, the six reasons why tourists come to Sri Lanka.

iii. Which method of planning and organising content points did you feel more comfortable with?

Paragraphing your summary

Paragraphing your summary is easy. Because it is a short piece of writing, it may be written in a single paragraph. In cases where there is more than one section to the rubric you may find it more logical to use each section to write a separate paragraph. But there is no need to do so – it is up to you. You will be neither penalised nor rewarded in an examination for the number of paragraphs which you use to write your summary. The same is not the case, of course, in continuous writing and directed writing, with which the section on Paper One in this book deals.

Exercise 3

Go back to Chapter 13 to the lists of content points you made for each of the short passages in Exercises 4, 5, 6, 7 and 8. For each of these, write the list of content points into a paragraph. Your paragraphs should be headed as follows:

• Cafe India

• Children in developing countries

• Children in developed countries

• A frightening experience

• Anna

Punctuating your summary

When you have produced a first draft, you must move quickly on to produce your final draft. The final draft is the one which will be assessed in an examination. Whether you have written your first draft in list or note form, or whether you have written it as a paragraph, your second draft must be written in formal continuous prose. Continuous prose means that it must be written in sentences and at least one paragraph, clearly punctuated. You probably know what is meant by formal writing, but some guidance on this will be given later.

The length of your summary

You will be told in the rubric the limit to the number of words you should use in your summary. You will be penalised for exceeding that limit; on the other hand, there is no benefit in writing much below the prescribed number of words, because if you use considerably fewer words than the number prescribed in the rubric, you will probably penalise yourself by not writing enough content points.

Correct punctuation

If you are working towards 'O' level English, it is assumed that you are familiar with the basic rules of punctuation, in other words that you can use full stops and capital letters accurately in order to produce correct sentences. You will already have done some work on sentence structure and punctuation in Chapter 3 of this book.

Exercise 4

Check your basic punctuation skills by redrafting the following passage using correct punctuation.

the moment had arrived all those weeks of preparation had been moving them towards this day o level english was a difficult syllabus but the class had had a good teacher how happy they were about that all the students filed into the examination hall with butterflies in their stomachs was there anyone who was not really nervous what would the comprehension passage be about this year would it be narrative or discursive would it suit everyone everyone was silent the papers were given out they were thinking about what they had been taught about literal comprehension and inferential comprehension not to forget of course the summary question which carried half of the marks everyone started to read the passage but they could not believe their eyes it was impossible to understand there was no punctuation whatsoever

Chapter

Writing summaries in Standard English in your own words

When you write your summary in your examination, you will be expected to write it in Standard English. You have already learned in Chapter 1 of this book, in Introduction to Paper One, that using Standard English means using the accepted conventions of expression and grammatical usage which are common to speakers and writers of English of all ages throughout the world. In your examination you will be given credit in your summary writing for the extent to which you write in Standard English.

If the sentence structures which you use are compound or complex but copied from the text, you will not get as much credit as you would if you wrote in original compound or complex sentence structures, that is sentence structures that have been created by you and not by the writer of the original passage. Obviously, writing original compound or complex sentence structures, as well as writing original simple structures, means using your own words. In your examination you will be given credit for your ability to use your own words as well as for your ability to write in Standard English.

Chapter 3 of this book, Key Writing Skills, gives definitions and examples of compound and complex sentences, as well as definitions and examples of main and subordinate clauses and the tools for creating complex sentences, including conjunctions, present participle phrases and relative pronouns. You are also given practice in joining up sentences and creating complex sentences in Chapter 3. If you are unsure of any of these terms – compound and complex sentences, main and subordinates clauses, conjunctions, present participial phrases, relative pronouns – it might be a good idea to refresh your memory by looking back at Chapter 3.

What follows is another opportunity to create original, complex sentences, which enhance the quality of the Standard English which you write, not only in Composition but also in Summary writing. In both Composition and Summary writing, a mark is allocated to the style of the writing which you produce.

Exercise 1 Conjunctions

Combine the following sentences by using conjunctions.

> i. Lucky was very tired. She had been studying sentence structure all day.
>
> ii. Lucky got home. Her mother was there to greet her.
>
> iii. Lucky ate her lunch. She went straight to her room to study.
>
> iv. Lucky revised that day's lesson on sentence structure. She felt very cheerful. She felt she understood how to use conjunctions.

Exercise 2 Relative Pronouns

Combine the following sentences by using relative pronouns.

> i. Tulen was an English teacher. He worked in a high school in Bangladesh.
>
> ii. Tulen taught English in a high school. The school had almost five hundred students.
>
> iii. Tulen met one of his former students. He had taught this student for three years of high school.
>
> iv. Tulen lived next door to Nath. He had taught Nath's son for two years of high school.

Exercise 3 Present Participles

Combine the following sentences by using present participles.

> i. Indrani walked to school. She met an old friend from high school.
>
> ii. They chatted together. They walked along the street.
>
> iii. Indrani heard that her friend was a teacher. She told her friend that she was a teacher too.
>
> iv. Her friend smiled. She told Indrani that she had heard from many colleagues that Indrani was a wonderful teacher.

Exercise 4 A Studying for an Examination

Combine the following list of summary content points to produce a paragraph of Standard English, with original complex sentence structures if possible. Write no more than 160 words, including the opening ten words given below.

Begin your answer like this:

Because Minhajul and Sajjad were students at the same school.

---

    i. Minhajul invited Sajjad to his house

   ii. spent three hours there on Saturday

  iii. English examination coming up

  iv. worried about sentence structure

   v. particularly worried about spelling

  vi. teacher had told them not to worry too much

 vii. examiners were kind about spelling

viii. examiners did not deduct marks for every single error

  ix. Minhajul and Sajjad were hungry

   x. they left their books on the table

  xi. they went to the kitchen

 xii. they drank some water

xiii. they ate some sandwiches

xiv. Minhajul's mother came in from the shops

 xv. she asked them how their studies were progressing

Exercise 4 B

Swap your answer with a partner. For your partner's summary:

- count the number of sentences
- check that they are all sentences. Do they all have verbs? Do they all make sense on their own?
- count the number of simple sentences, i.e. sentences with only one verb.
- check to see if there are any compound sentences, i.e. sentences joined by 'and' or 'but'.
- check to see if there are any complex sentences, and whether or not these are original.

- for each complex sentence used, check the way in which the structure has been created
- has a conjunction been used? ('because', 'when', 'after', 'before', 'since' etc.)
- has a relative pronoun been used ('who', 'whose', 'whom', 'which' ,'that')
- has a present participle been used? (the part of the verb ending in 'ing' e.g. 'going', 'seeing')
- have linking words been used appropriately ('however', 'moreover', 'nevertheless', 'furthermore' etc.)

Make a list of your findings for your partner. Your partner will be doing the same with your piece of work.

Exercise 4 C

Take your own piece of work back from your partner. Study carefully what your partner has written. Redraft your summary, trying to make the necessary corrections and/or improvements to it as suggested by your partner.

Exercise 5 A   A New Job in Male

Combine the following list of summary content points to produce a paragraph of Standard English, with original complex sentence structures if possible. Write no more than 160 words, including the opening ten words given below.

Begin your answer like this: The flight from Pakistan was long and exhausting for Amrita...

   i. Amrita was a mathematics teacher.

  ii. she was pleased to have a job in Male'

 iii. she arrived in Male' by boat from the airport

  iv. she checked into her new lodgings

   v. she went for a walk to see her new surroundings

  vi. she went to the fish market

 vii. tuna was the main fish caught and sold

viii. they lay around on the floor of the market

  ix. there was a strong smell of fish

x. and a lot a noise

xi. shoppers were mainly women

xii. the women selected the tuna they wanted

xiii. and took it to the salesmen and it was weighed and paid for

xiv. Amrita bought a piece of tuna

xv. she went back to her lodgings to have the tuna for supper

Exercise 5 B

Swap your answer with a partner. For your partner's summary:

- count the number of sentences
- check that they are all sentences. Do they all have verbs? Do they all make sense on their own?
- count the number of simple sentences, i.e. sentences with only one verb
- check to see if there are any compound sentences, i.e. sentences joined by 'and' or 'but'
- check to see if there are any complex sentences, and whether or not these are original
- for each complex sentence used, check the way in which the structure has been created
- has a conjunction been used? ('because', 'when', 'after', 'before', 'since' etc.)
- has a relative pronoun been used ('who', 'whose', 'whom', 'which' ,'that')
- has a present participle been used? (the part of the verb ending in 'ing' e.g. 'going', 'seeing')
- have linking words been used appropriately ('however', 'moreover', 'nevertheless', 'furthermore' etc.)

Make a list of your findings for your partner. Your partner will be doing the same with your piece of work.

Exercise 5 C

Take your own piece of work back from your partner. Study carefully what your partner has written. Redraft your summary, trying to make the necessary corrections and/or improvements to it as suggested by your partner.

Exercise 6 A Light Street and Heavy Street

Combine the following list of summary content points to produce a paragraph of Standard English, with original complex sentence structures if possible. Write no more than 160 words, including the opening ten words given below.

Begin your answer like this: The volume of traffic in streets produces contrasts between them...

i. in Light Street (street with light traffic) people consider the street as home territory

ii. in Heavy Street (street with heavy traffic) only the building they live in is considered as home

iii. in Light Street people make use of the street

iv. people sit on the front steps and chat in Light Street

v. children play on the pavements in Light Street

vi. Heavy Street is seen as a corridor between the safety of individual homes and the outside world

vii. there is no community feeling in Heavy Street

viii. people keep to themselves in Heavy Street

ix. in Heavy Street motorists view pedestrians, cyclists or children playing in the street as intruding into their space

x. as the speed of the traffic increases in Heavy Street the attitude of motorists to pedestrians become increasingly ruthless

xi. In Heavy Street the pavement eventually disappears

xii. there are no more pedestrians or children playing in the street

xiii. the pavement becomes a no-man's land and the street loses its main attraction

xiv. people on Heavy Street no longer use their front gardens.

xv. they cannot relax in their gardens because of the continual noise

Exercise 6 B

Swap your answer with a partner. For your partner's summary:

- count the number of sentences
- check that they are all sentences. Do they all have verbs? Do they all make sense on their own?
- count the number of simple sentences, i.e. sentences with only one verb.
- check to see if there are any compound sentences, i.e. sentences joined by 'and' or 'but'
- check to see if there are any complex sentences and whether or not these are original
- for each complex sentence used, check the way in which the structure has been created
- has a conjunction been used? ('because', 'when', 'after', 'before', 'since' etc.)
- has a relative pronoun been used ('who', 'whose', 'whom', 'which' ,'that')
- has a present participle been used? (the part of the verb ending in 'ing' e.g. 'going', 'seeing')
- have linking words been used appropriately ('however', 'moreover', 'nevertheless', 'furthermore' etc.)

Make a list of your findings for your partner. Your partner will be doing the same with your piece of work.

Exercise 6 C

Take your own piece of work back from your partner. Study carefully what your partner has written. Redraft your summary, trying to make the necessary corrections and / or improvements to it as suggested by your partner.

Exercise 7 A   The Changing Relationship Between Man and Animals

Combine the following list of summary content points to produce a paragraph of Standard English, with original complex sentence structures if possible. Write no more than 160 words, including the opening ten words given below.

Begin your answer like this: The farming of wild animals produced various changes in their...

i. the physical appearance of farmed animals changed

ii. most farmed animals became smaller

iii. some farmed animals developed more distinctive markings and /or bright colours

iv. the jaw muscles in grazing animals became smaller

v. the faces of grazing animals became shorter

vi. the brains of farmed animals became smaller

vii. the senses of farmed animals became less acute

viii. before the farming of animals, man respected the animals he hunted

ix. Man depended on animals for his needs, like food and clothing

x. the bones of animals became the weapons of man

xi. hunters feared and admired the animals they hunted

xii. in some societies animals were idolised as gods

xiii. farming certain species of animals led to a bond of mutual affection between them and the farmers

xiv. shepherds often risked their lives to rescue their lambs

xv. dogs and horses became inseparable companions of their masters

Exercise 7 B

Swap your answer with a partner. For your partner's summary:

- count the number of sentences

- check that they are all sentences. Do they all have verbs? Do they all make sense on their own?

- count the number of simple sentences, i.e. sentences with only one verb.

- check to see if there are any compound sentences, i.e. sentences joined by 'and' or 'but'

- check to see if there are any complex sentences, and whether or not these are original

- for each complex sentence used, check the way in which the structure has been created

- has a conjunction been used? ('because', 'when', 'after', 'before', 'since' etc.)

- has a relative pronoun been used ('who', 'whose', 'whom', 'which' ,'that')
- has a present participle been used? (the part of the verb ending in 'ing' e.g. 'going', 'seeing')
- have linking words been used appropriately ('however', 'moreover', 'nevertheless', 'furthermore' etc.)

Make a list of your findings for your partner. Your partner will be doing the same with your piece of work.

Exercise 7 C

Take your own piece of work back from your partner. Study carefully what your partner has written. Redraft your summary, trying to make the necessary corrections and / or improvements to it as suggested by your partner.

Exercise 8 A

Make up your own list of summary points. These can be of a narrative nature or a discursive nature. There should be fifteen points and you should provide the ten opening words.

Exercise 8 B

Swap your list of content points with your partner. Write a summary based on the content points your partner has given you. Use the opening ten words your partner has provided. Write no more than 160 words, including the ten opening words. Write in formal continuous prose. Try to use a variety of sentence structures, some simple and some complex. Check your spelling and punctuation. Check that you have created complex sentences by the use of present participles or conjunctions or relative pronouns.

Exercise 8 C

Swap your work again with your partner. Write a short paragraph about the summary your partner has produced with the content points you gave him/ her. Assess the extent to which he/ she has written error free prose and the extent to which he / she has used a variety of sentence structures.

Exercise 9

Look at what your partner has written about your summary, the good points and the points which might be improved. Decide how your work on summary writing in formal, continuous prose might be improved in the future.

Chapter **28**

More Standard English

Each exercise which follows gives you a first draft summary. For each one, produce a redrafted version. This means you will have to:

- correct any mistakes of grammar, punctuation, agreement, wrong preposition, spelling
- insert links, (e.g. 'however' or 'furthermore') where appropriate
- combine groups of simple sentences into complex or compound sentences where appropriate
- redraft legibly and in your best handwriting

    Remember that Assessment Objective (xii) is to write legibly, and present finished work clearly and attractively. You may in fact lose marks in the examination for handwriting which is illegible or difficult to read.

Exercise 1 Pavlo 1

It was important for Pavlo to be warm and so we turned up the heating to its highest. We massaged Pavlo body with warm olive oil. He lay on cushion, wrapped in a cotton wool for warmth. We carry him to garden every time the sun shines. We gave him a bottled filled with hot water in his bed and night. We give him a drawer in a cabinet in my room which includes a piece of fur on which he would curl up. In early morning, Pavlo keep running in every room to find a better way to keep him warm. He liked to crawl inside the shade and sit next to bulb which is in sitting room, he enjoyed drinking warm milk. In winter we have to be carefull to ensure that the windows was close to preventing Pavlo to be caught in cold In the first warm days in spring, Pavlo went into the garden.

Exercise 2 Pavlo 2

It was important for Pavlo to be warm and so that he would not felt the diffrence of the climate from South America. It also played part for the health of the marmoset. As the prophecies of the animal was going to realised within six months, the family started to take it seriously by surrounded his place of cotton wool for warmth. Olive oil was also to keep the tiny body of Pavlo warm, by making little and cautious massage that the family done they also put his cushion in every patch of sunlight, to help him sleep at the night, they gave him a bottle filled with hot water during cold winter also in summer. The family had to push drawer close for extra warmth the writer's sister even bought a baby blanket for Pavlo to keep him warm and he like to jump in, searching for heat. Between the plenty of heating they had, Pavlo preferred the electric lamp.

Exercise 3   The Lighthouse 1

The ship's crew noticed immediately that something was wrong because there were no welcoming flag from lighthouse when the ship is near. Whistle and rocket are used, still there is no response from those lighthouse keepers. The gates that should be open was close, the door of the lighthouse was widely open. The fire had not being lit for some time. The last entery of the lighthouse record book were the fifteenth of december, this puzzled the searchers. The lamp covering with dust showing that it also had not been lit for some time, the beds was unmade. Two of the three sets waterproof clothing was missing from cupboard. The grass along the edge of cliff was torn away when they investigate outside the lighthouse. The railings around the platform where the crane stood was broken. A huge boulder which was part of cliff had been move a great distance down the starecase and blocking it.

Exercise 4   The Lighthouse 2

The ship's crew noticed immediately that something was wrong because the welcoming flag should be wave for our welcome. They thought that the keepers may busy working out of sight. The wistle was blown to call the keeper but no responce. The ship's captain order his crew to fired a rocked but it didn't make the keepers noticed. A small group of sailor was ordered to check the area. They found out that the warning lamp was working order and when they check the record book, it haven't been filled for 11 days. The sailor told their captain that they didn't found the keepers, the next day they search the lighthouse and found out that two of the three waterproof clothing was missing. The railing around the platform was broken and huge boulder was move down stairway. There were no trace of the three keepers later than. All the crew of the ships thinks there a mystery their.

Exercise 5   The Lighthouse 3

The ship's crew noticed immediately that something was wrong because there was no welcoming flag flew from the ashore. The captain asked to fly a rocket over the island but still nothing was seen of the keepers. Some sailors are order to find what happend inshore, they started calling the keepers names and there is no answers. The enterance gate were closed, it should be open by the keepers as they came there. The main door was open and again calling the name of the keeper. In the kitchen too chairs stood next to the table and one of it knocked over and lying on it's side. The bedroom were unmade seems that the occupants had just risen from them and left hurriedly. There is a this dirty dust over the warning lamp. They found two waterproof clothing were missing and one still hung there. They also found that the grass had been torn away along top edge of cliff.

Exercise 6   Threats To Coral Reefs 1

When hotel developers near coral reefs compete for land, thus raise it's price and as result forced local people to leave thier homes. Infact, in some places, hotels have been built on burial sites on the coast. Little by little the construction of golf courses for tourists have been proved fatal to the coral reefs as the golf courses are treated by fertilisers, pesticides and large amount of water when all of substences contains deadly loads of waste materials and chemical. However, airport runways are built and thos its construction produces to much waste which are sufficient to kill coral. Local people lacking of food caused by the distruction of coral. Even, the increase of pollution, noice, raods and the destruction of natural habitats of animals from the arrival of tourists. Sailing ships create severe on coral reefs with their heavy anchor, coral continues to damage from the submarines power and diver also damage coral reefs considerably.

Exercise 7   Threats to Coral Reefs 2

When hotel develops near coral reefs compete for land they force local people out of their homes, it is easy to understand the location of hotels in this magnificent areas but way of live of country is exploitd to great extent. Tourist attractions like golf coarses deprives the local people for shorelines which is necesary for their way of life. Pollution is important factor in the destruction of wonderful coastal areas. Pollutants is dumped into the coral reefs which destroy life in the reef, the rock from coral reef have been use on a small scale to build houses but the rocks are now been excavated in large quantities for hotel development and yet again depriving the local people from their own houses. Lagoons are being dig deeper affecting the area where fish breed and the prices of popular fish has been raised so high that the people cannot aford them, boats that carry people cases severe damage to reefs.

Exercise 8 Threats to Coral Reefs 3

When hotel develops compete for land they forced local people out of their homes, the country is frequently exploit for tourist entertainment. The construction of golf courses for tourists deprive local people of coastal area. The water used by golf courses drains out on the coral reefs carries deadly load and chemical, building of airport along the coast are built on coral reefs. Their construction produce large quantities of waste. Rock from coral reef are taken in uncontroled quantities to built tourist hotel thus depriving local people of building material. Pleasure boat distroy the areas were fish breed, deprives local people's food. Some fish are too expensive because they can only afford by tourist. Villages are destroyed by pollution created by tourists. Huge jetties and docks is built over coral reefs, Hotel often lack of proper sewage facilities. Boats carrying people to dive. These boats increases the destruction of coral. Everyday boats send there anchors crashing down on reef.

Chapter **29**

Choosing vocabulary suited to its purpose

Assessment Objective (x) in 'O' level English Language is testing your ability to choose a vocabulary which is suited to its purpose and audience. You have an opportunity to consider appropriate vocabulary, tone and register in earlier chapters in this book which deal with composition writing. The matter of vocabulary, tone and register is more complex in Paper 1 of your examination than it is in Paper 2. This is because you might be writing to amuse or entertain, or to persuade and argue, or to reflect on past events; you might be writing a letter, or a report, where the purpose and audience is given in the rubric of directed writing.

However, choosing vocabulary suited to its purpose is much simpler in Paper 2. You might be relieved to know that in comprehension questions you are being tested on reading rather than writing, and so there are no penalties for the wrong type of vocabulary (provided, of course, that the sense is clear), tone or register. The area of Paper 2 where vocabulary, tone and register become important is the summary question, and this is relatively straightforward because the golden rule is formality.

A definition of formal language is probably best given by a definition of what it is not. Signposts of informal language are chatty or conversational language or tone, abbreviations or contractions, the active rather than the reported voice of the verb and the use of direct speech. So, signposts of formal language could be seen as being:

- no chatty or conversational language or tone, e.g. It is clear to see that...' rather than 'Let's be clear about...'

- no abbreviations or contractions, e.g. 'Coral reefs cannot be looked after if...' rather than 'Coral reefs can't be looked after...

- the passive rather than the active voice of the verb, e.g. 'It can be seen that...' rather than 'I can see that...'

- no direct speech, e.g. 'The captain said that the crew should go to the lighthouse', rather than 'I am going to the lighthouse,' the captain said.

- no slang or colloquial expressions, e.g. 'The children thought that their teacher was efficient and friendly', rather than 'The kids thought that their teacher was cool'.

Exercise 1

Working with a partner, look at (i) a copy of a novel, either your own or from the class or school library and (ii) a more formal text of your own choice, which can be a non-fiction text such as an instruction manual, an autobiography or a book designed to give information on a particular topic. Write down ten examples of informal language and ten examples of formal language. Beside each example, write a sentence or two to explain why your choice of example is either formal or informal language.

Frequently asked questions

Question 1

Will I be penalised if my summary has more than the number of words indicated in the rubric?

Answer

The examiner will not deduct marks for a summary which exceeds the number of words indicated in the rubric. However, the examiner will put a line through the excess words and not even read them. Thus, you will have penalised yourself because any content points in the excess words will not be credited.

Question 2

Will I be penalised if my summary is too short?

Answer

Yes, but again it will be a case of penalising yourself. If the rubric specifies 160 words as the maximum, excluding the opening ten given words, you should try to write as near to that as possible, because if you write fewer than this number, it is unlikely you will make enough content points. It is difficult enough to score fifteen content points in 160 words – doing it in 120 words is impossible.

In addition, a short answer will not be given the same mark for the style of writing. Because you are more likely to make mistakes in 160 words than in, say, 100 words, it is only fair to reduce the style mark for short answers. Besides, because you cannot show your ability to use original complex sentence structures in 100 words as you could do in 160 words, you would penalise yourself in short answers.

Question 3

Will the examiner count the number of words I have written?

Answer

Yes. All summaries are checked for the number of words used. Examiners make sure that the rubric 'not more than' is adhered to. The only way in which this can be done is by counting the words.

Question 4

Can I save on words by 'contracting' e.g. by using 'can't' instead of 'can not'?

Answer

No. The examiner will count 'can't' as two separate words, and so you gain nothing. Remember that your summary is meant to be a piece of formal prose, and there is no place in formal prose for informal language such as contractions.

Question 5

Will I be penalised if I forget to write the number of words used at the end of my summary?

Answer

No. Nevertheless, you will want to know for yourself how many words are in your summary, so that you write neither too short nor too long a summary. Therefore, it is good practice to write down the number of words used.

Question 6

Will I be penalised if I do not use the ten opening words supplied in the question?

No. However, you will again penalise yourself. The opening ten words are specifically to lead you into the first available content point. Also, if you do not use them, the examiner will count the first word of your summary as the eleventh word, and so you have not gained an extra ten words for your content points.

Question 7

Does it matter if my summary is one single paragraph or several?

Unless the rubric specifies a particular number of paragraphs for your summary – which is rather unusual – you may write more than one if you wish. However, the nature of the task, and the relatively short run of words required, mean that for practical purposes you will probably need only one paragraph.

Question 8

Will I get credit for an answer written in note form?

Your summary is marked both for content points and for style. If within a note form answer you have made content points in full, you will gain marks for them in the normal way. However, you will automatically gain no marks for style. It is clearly not a good idea to write in note form.

Question 9

If the rubric specifies that my summary should be written in the third person (i.e. 'he', 'she' and 'they') will I be penalised if I write in the first person (i.e. 'I' and 'we')?

Answer

There is no set penalty for this error. But if you forget to take the rubric into consideration, it will be taken into account when the style of your writing is assessed. Usually, it counts as a single error; you won't be penalised for the same error over and over again. However, it is an error and it is always best to obey the rubric.

(The passage describes how a little boy, Joseph, gets lost on a shopping trip with his mother.)

The pirate king, wearing a fancy white shirt, a scarlet velvet jacket and long black boots, had an aggressive expression on his face and a sharp, shiny sword in his hand. Enchanted, Joseph studied the picture in his story book. The letters danced before his eyes as he tried to recall the words of the story his mother had read to him the previous night, before she had tucked him into bed and kissed him goodnight.

'Joseph!' his mother exclaimed, bustling impatiently into the room. 'It's time to go into town to buy you new clothes for starting school. Are you pleased?' Without waiting for an answer, she hurriedly ushered him out of the front door in the direction of the bus stop. Reluctantly, Joseph trailed along behind her. He was the pirate king. He had a mission: adventures to complete and enemies to confront. He brightened a little as the bus came bumping and rattling over the hill, because this was his pirate ship dipping and rising with the turbulence of the ocean. His mother clasped his hand tightly and directed him to a seat. On the journey she counted the contents of her purse, anxious in case her own mission might not be successful. When the bus reached the shopping centre, Joseph found himself propelled onto the pavement and led into a store.

With a practised eye, Joseph's mother scanned the rails of children's clothes, checking sizes and prices, and picked out trousers, shirts and a jacket. Hiding her irritation at his indifference to the shopping trip, she coaxed him to co-operate with her by promising a reward at the end of it – a small toy, perhaps, or some fruit. 'Please be a good boy, Joseph. I don't know what's got into you today!' she complained, as her son's aggressive face stared back at her from the mirror in the changing room. Joseph's young conscience was stirred by this, and he decided to try looking on the bright side. Maybe the jacket wasn't scarlet or velvet, but at least the shirts were white, if rather plain, and black trousers were probably acceptable for pirate kings. Before long, the transaction was complete, and his new school clothes were put into plastic bags.

'Kim! It's so long since I saw you! How are you?' Joseph recognised the former neighbour who greeted his mother at the store counter. He shuffled from foot to foot as the two women gave their respective accounts of the past two years, until suddenly his attention was seized by a picture which he had until now failed to notice on the wall of this children's section of the store. He could hardly believe his eyes – there, complete with mast and white sails, was the pirate ship of his story book.

As if under a magnetic force, he slipped his hand free of his mother's and moved towards the picture. He stared at it, wondering whether the pirate king was in his cabin or had gone ashore. He wandered through into the next section of the store and discovered that this was the toy department. He gazed at furry bears, model cars and plastic dinosaurs piled up in a delightful display; best of all, on a huge table two miniature trains ran round on a track, passing under bridges and past toy stations. Joseph stared longingly at these for several minutes, but, being an inquisitive child, and still thinking of himself as the pirate king ashore, he set off for further exploration. Downstairs, he strolled through the section of the store selling household goods. A fascinated crowd had gathered to listen to a salesman demonstrating the efficiency of a kitchen knife which resembled a sharp, shiny sword. As the salesman talked, peelings from various fruits fell to the floor in unbroken loops. Had the demonstration been less enthralling, someone might have noticed a small boy slipping through the front door and out into the busy street.

A band of amateur musicians had congregated outside the store and Joseph studied them with interest. Two women in colourful dresses played wind instruments, while their equally colourful male companions beat drums and moved through their audience, collecting coins as donations. Joseph squeezed through the crowd and moved further down the street. He came across a beggar sitting by the side of the road. A small can with some coins in it was placed near his feet, but there the similarity with the musicians ended. His clothes were dull, drab and tattered, and Joseph looked at him warily before hurrying on. He loitered at a roadside stall selling snacks to passing shoppers and listened to the friendly exchanges between the young cook – a boy wearing an alarmingly grubby apron – and his customers. Nearby, at a small shop selling bales of cloth piled to the ceiling, Joseph stared at the fabrics which were in almost every colour imaginable – reds, blues, yellows, purples. Emerging from the tiny doorway of the shop was a young boy accompanied by his mother, who held his hand tightly. At once, a panic clutched at Joseph's heart, making him breathless with fear: where was his own mother? His pirate king adventures forgotten, he turned round and round in the street, looking for her, but with no success. All that met his gaze were strange buildings, strange people, strange shops. The brave pirate king started to cry, tears spouting from his eyes, his sobs so loud and uncontrollable that they soon produced a flurry of interest from passers-by.

Meanwhile, Kim had enjoyed her chat with her former neighbour and they parted amicably, having made an arrangement to meet up at a later date. 'Goodbye, I'll see you soon,' cried Kim, turning round to take her son home. But where was he? Suppressing the urge to panic, she tried to be rational. Why would a five-year-old wander away from his mother? Why would he want to go far? She retraced her steps to the rails of children's clothes, trying to remain calm. He must be playing or hiding in the changing area, she thought, and checked out that theory. At this point her thinly disguised terror caused her to be noticed by a store assistant, who escorted her to an office. 'Please wait here until I find the manager,' was the instruction. Kim paced the small office impatiently, filled with guilt and fear.

After what seemed an eternity the manager arrived, trying to reassure Kim that all would be well. 'Already I have sent several members of staff out into the street to look for Joseph; in any case, a small boy cannot go far in a matter of minutes. Nevertheless, I have telephoned the police.' And so, at the same time as Joseph, Kim began to cry, but not for long. Realising that practicality was preferable to hysteria, she accompanied the manager to the store entrance. How long it seemed since she had brought Joseph through that door! As she stood helplessly looking up and down the street, she suddenly noticed two young women wearing the store's uniform approaching her and, to her great joy and relief, each was holding the hand of a small boy .... Joseph! Kim ran towards him, scooping him up into her arms, and the pirate king allowed himself to be embraced.

On the bus back to their village, Joseph stayed close by his mother. Once inside the house again, Kim and Joseph carefully hung up the new school clothes in the cupboard. Over dinner, Joseph was uncharacteristically withdrawn. Noting the change in her son, Kim offered to read to him from one of his story books.

'What about this one?' she asked, holding up the story of the pirate king.

'No, another one,' replied Joseph firmly, taking the book from his mother and placing it face downwards on the shelf.

Read the passage in the insert and then answer **all** the questions which follow below.

You are recommended to answer the questions in the order set.

Mistakes in spelling, punctuation and grammar may be penalised in any part of the Paper.

From paragraph 1:

1. How does the writer suggest that Joseph has not yet learned to read? [1]

From paragraph 2:

2. (a) Joseph's mother ushered him 'hurriedly' out of the front door. In what two other ways did her behaviour suggest she was in a hurry? [2]

(b) Joseph's mother was 'anxious in case her own mission might not be successful'. What exactly was she worried about? [1]

From paragraph 3:

3. Pick out and write down the single word which shows that Joseph's mother was treating him very tactfully. [1]

From paragraph 4:

4. Explain **in your own words** what Joseph's mother and her former neighbour were doing as Joseph 'shuffled from foot to foot'. [2]

From paragraph 5:

5. (a) What does the word 'magnetic' tell us about the effect of the picture on Joseph? [1]

(b) Of all the toys for sale, which did Joseph find most attractive? [1]

(c) Joseph, we are told, was 'an inquisitive child'. What other reason is suggested for his decision to 'set off for further exploration'? [1]

(d) Why did nobody in the household goods department notice Joseph leaving the store? [1]

From paragraph 6:

6. (a) What did the beggar and the musicians have in common? [1]

   (b) Why should it be 'alarming' that the boy was wearing a grubby apron? [1]

From paragraph 7:

7. (a) Explain **in your own words** why Joseph's mother was noticed by the store assistant. [2]

   (b) Joseph's mother was afraid for his safety. Why do you think she was also 'filled with guilt'? [1]

From paragraph 8:

8. Because he was glad to see his mother again, 'the pirate king allowed himself to be embraced'. What else do you think the writer is suggesting about Joseph's feelings at this point? [1]

From paragraph 9:

9. (a) Explain **in your own words** the change which Kim noticed in her son. [2]

   (b) Why did Joseph place the book 'face downwards on the shelf'? [1]

From the whole passage:

10. Choose **five** of the following words or phrases. For each of them give **one** word or short phrase (of not more than **seven** words) which has the same meaning that the word or phrase has in the passage.

enchanted (line 2)	congregated (line 42)
reluctantly (line 8)	suppressing (line 61)
with a practised eye (line 15)	rational (line 62)
efficiency (line 38)	firmly (line 82) [5]

11. **Using your own words as far as possible**, write a summary of what Joseph did when he left his mother, the steps that were taken to find him, and how he was eventually re-united with his mother.

USE ONLY THE MATERIAL FROM LINE 30 TO LINE 76

Your summary, which must be in continuous writing (not note form) must not be longer than **160** words, including the **10** words given below.

Begin your summary as follows:

After Joseph had let go of his mother's hand he...   [25]

Answer Key

All answers are worth 1 mark unless otherwise stated

Chapter 11 Reading a variety of texts
Exercise 3

Fiction: 2, 4, 5, 6, 7, 9

Non-fiction: 1, 3, 8, 10

Chapter 12 More exercises in fact gathering from short texts
Exercise 1 Joseph

  i.   Joseph intimidated him / got better marks than he did

 ii.   pleased

iii.   he liked him

 iv.   he was good company / had quirky sense of humour / was thoughtful/ kindhearted

  v.   he was clever

Exercise 2 Stamford Raffles

  i.   sea captain

 ii.   his father got into debt

iii.   clerk in the office of the East India Company

 iv.   the office hours were long

  v.   sometimes he couldn't afford candles for his night reading

 vi.   it was well-paid

Exercise 3 Maids and their employers

  i.   television programmes

 ii.   laziness / argue over what maids will or will not do / attitudes / behaviour

iii.   cruelty and deprivation

 iv.   employers

Exercise 4 Anna

  i. the bus was crowded when it arrived

 ii. the market

iii. the stall selling clothing material

 iv. dress for herself or shirt for father

  v. the caves (near the market)

 vi. No, she was not allowed

Exercise 5 Modern Travel

  i. ordinary people can travel more

 ii. shorter working week

iii. they can travel further

 iv. they cut back on extra services

  v. affluence / money

 vi. travel

Exercise 6 Gerry

  i. his alarm didn't ring/ the battery in his alarm needed replaced

 ii. pack his bag the night before / leave an organised bag at the front door

iii. school bus

 iv. he missed the bus

  v. he was hungry

 vi. it was not appropriate for a boy of his age

Exercise 7 The Intruder

  i. break into / rob a house

 ii. so that he wouldn't later be identified

iii. dressed in a nondescript way / wore a baseball cap over his eyes

 iv. it was a deserted part of town

  v. four

 vi. the owner/ husband /father

vii. Tuesday

viii. a bag of tools

Chapter 13 Selecting and retrieving information

Exercise 1

Literal : 1, 2, 4, 7, 9

Inferential: 3, 5, 6, 8, 10

Exercise 2 City Life

i. Advantages: access to work / services / education / entertainment / friends (any for 1 mark) Disadvantages: traffic / cost of living / crime (any for 1 mark)

ii. difference in property values / deterioration in public services

Exercise 3 Classroom Computers

i. deterioration in educational standards

ii. computers

iii. computers will become a substitute for teachers

iv. it brings together the best work of teachers and students

Exercise 4 Inferential Questions

i. there would be fewer people to pay for services

ii. kids: young people having fun (round a computer) [1]
students: young people taking education seriously / receiving good education [1]

Exercise 6 Exploring a Cave

i. the damp / dusty smell

ii. (light casts) eerie / frightening shadows on the wall

iii. he wouldn't see the roof [1] and he would bang his head [1]

iv. pain in the knees

v. getting to the end (1) and getting back [1]

vi. he would be tired

vii. rocks could hurt his feet [1] and he could walk into pools of water [1]

Exercise 7 Valladolid

 i. there was no-one around / it was (almost) dark / the light was mysterious // it was an unknown city / he had never been there before // he had nowhere to stay (any 2 for 1 mark each)

 ii. find a place to stay

 iii. everything / the furniture had been devastated / destroyed by previous visitors

 iv. the landlord was unpleasant/ unfriendly [1] there was no furniture / only a bed [1]

 v. a boy singing

 vi. shouts / knocking on the door

 vii. it was sudden / loud / annoying / violent (any 2 for 1 mark each)

Chapter 14 More exercises in literal and inferential comprehension

Exercise 1 Julia

 i. late childbirth [1] / trying to please her husband [1]

 ii. fifteen

 iii. he tried to make her departure unpleasant

 iv. she had a scholarship

 v. she could never face living with another man

 vi. she had taken her for granted [1] / she had not treated her as well as she might [1]

 vii. without thinking things through

 viii. because she had learned to love someone else

 ix. you don't know you're lonely

 x. to stress Julia's loneliness

Exercise 2 Selling the Flat

 i. sell her flat

 ii. he invited her in [1] / gestured hospitably [1] / made her tea [1]

 iii. garden looks seedy

 iv. the turf was parched

v. The ducks were bedraggled

vi. the sum Mr Akbar was offering was low

vii. ask for more / tell him he wasn't offering enough

viii. Mr Akbar's eyes were pleading

ix. she had bought the flat for a good price

x. it had been Mr Akbar's suggestion to buy the flat [1] / Mr Akbar didn't look wealthy [1]

Exercise 3   Easter Island

i. they share a common ancestor

ii. shaped less by nature and more by culture

iii. we have become creatures of our own making

iv. our experiment on material progress began to expand and accelerate

v. we will blow up or degrade the biosphere [1] so that it can no longer sustain us [1]

vi. history is often edited

vii. it helps us to uncover deeds we have accidentally forgotten [1] or choose to forget [1]

viii. it was so treeless and eroded

ix. Captain Cook and his crew were Dutch

x. there was no wood or fresh water

xi. machinery/ cranes / supports

xii. there were huge statues there [1] but no sign of life / of their builders [1]

xiii. pollen studies

Chapter 15 Selecting and retrieving information by lifting

Exercise 1   Coral Reefs

i. it is beautiful / teeming with life / set among a rich and random pattern of colours

ii. coral reefs are second only to rain forests in the huge number of plants and animals they support.

iii. Just as forest plants have been used for hundreds of years for medicinal purposes by people living in the rain forests, so some reef plants and animal have been used by people in coastal communities to help cure diseases like malaria.

Chapter 2 Grandfather

   i. he read her stories

   ii. his voice was gruff

  iii. his skin was wrinkly (and she liked to trace with her eye particular lines as they meandered from one side of his face to the other)

  iv. she had to sit very still as his clothes were scratchy and made her legs red if she move too much

Exercise 3 Jennifer

   i. spending a day with an old friend

   ii. first day at primary school

  iii. local youth club / walked / talked / went shopping

  iv. it made her reflect on the nature of real friendship – having someone value you for what you are.

Exercise 4 Chris

   i. his friend was a doctor

   ii. his build was neither slim nor athletic

  iii. he had committed himself to raising money for charity

  iv. running on the pavements around his home [1] / he sweated on the treadmill in his local gym [1]

   v. he had had a great tour of London

Chapter 16 More exercises in lifting

Exercise 1 Grandfather's Study

   i. in Grandfather's study, mounted butterflies and moths had disintegrated (into small heaps of iridescent dust that powdered the bottom of their glass display cases)

   ii. glass display cases

  iii. the room was rank with fungus and disease / dirty glass panes / dust on the floor

  iv. the floor

v. dragged to the bookshelf

iv. dragged to the table and lifted on to it

vii. the leather binding had lifted off each book and buckled (like corrugated asbestos) [1] insects tunnelled through the pages (burrowing arbitrarily from species to species, turning organised information into yellow lace) [1]

viii. Rahel groped behind the row of books

ix. (they were) hidden [1] and wrapped in clear plastic and stuck with sellotape [1]

Exercise 2 The Brazilian Rain Forest

i. the skies of Western Brazil grow dark by day (as well as by night)

ii. to clear land for crop growing and cattle rearing

iii. They burn down vast areas

iv. scientists see this great annual destruction as a major peril for Brazil [1] and also for the rest of the world [1]

v. Politicians have joined scientists to try to stop the foolish waste of the precious resources of the planet.

vi. No, because for more than four hundred years settlers and farmers have been attacking Brazil's forests

vii. The feature is that the jungles are seemingly indestructible, [1] and the evidence he gives is that their power of recovery defeated their efforts [1]

viii. areas larger than some whole countries have been permanently stripped bare.

ix. they cut down trees

x. the forests contain an astonishing variety of animal and plant life which is slowly but surely disappearing

Exercise 3 Estha and Rahel

i. to hospital (in Shillong)

ii. they flagged down a (crowded State Transport) bus

iii. the passengers were poor and the parents were rich

iv. they saw how hugely pregnant Ammu was

v. to prevent it from wobbling

vi. they'd have got free bus rides for the rest of their lives

vii. it wasn't clear where he's got this information from

viii. for having diddled them out of a lifetime of free bus rides

ix. the Government would pay for their funerals

x. there were no zebra crossings to get killed on in Ayamenem

Exercise 4 The Domestication of Animals

i. it takes special qualities to make animals suitable for domestication

ii. so that her milk can be used for human consumption

iii. they must be able to find food for themselves

iv. they must breed freely in captivity

v. (i) food (ii) clothing (iii) transport

vi. (It could have come) naturally from Man's experience as a nomadic hunter

vii. (i) low-growing plants appeared then (ii) grass

viii. there was wild game in abundance

ix. as he followed his prey on their yearly migrations he gradually began to influence their movements and behaviour

x. they could more easily be rounded up and some of them slaughtered

xi. they were encouraged to become part of the community / pets

Chapter 17 Evaluating information

Exercise 1

i. HORRIFIED: shocked DEVASTATION: destruction

ii. CRAWLED: moved slowly (smoke) BILLOWED: blew

iii. DETERIORATION: worsening LITERACY: reading and writing

iv. IN PROFUSION: plentifully COILED: wound

v. DISREGARDED: ignored VIEWS: opinions

vi. INEVITABLE: unavoidable DESTRUCTION: wasting

vii. MOUNTING: increasing ASTONISHMENT: surprise

viii. EXHILARATING: exciting TERRIFYING: very frightening

ix. MANUFACTURE (tool): make ADORN: decorate

x. INITIATED: begun SUPERVISED: guided

Exercise 2

i. INQUISITIVE: curious (not) FRIGHTENED: afraid

ii. IMMOBILITY: (they did) not move

Exercise 3

i. FALSE: he was pretending INDIFFERENCE: not to care

Exercise 4

i. UNCONVINCING: difficult to believe SPECULATION: guessing

ii. CONCLUSIVELY: finally SOLVED: worked out

iii. LESS FANCIFUL: not so [1] imaginative [1]

iv. REPAIR: put right DEVASTATION: destruction INCLEMENT: bad

Exercise 5

i. GREATER: more VARIETY: different types

ii. LABOUR: work EXTRACT: get out

iii. DEFIED IMITATION: could not be [1] copied[1]

iv. INCREASINGLY (large): growing QUANTITIES: amounts

v. VALUE: worth DIMINISHED: grew smaller

Chapter 18 More exercises in own words questions

Exercise 1 Pavlo

i. STALK: follow CONSPICUOUS: easily seen

ii. (garden lost its) APPEAL: attraction

iii. QUIRKY (personality): STRANGE AFFECTIONATE (nature): loving

Exercise 2 Man and Animals

i. STRENGTH: power SPEED: swiftness SUPERIOR: better (than others)

ii. RELATIONSHIP: involvement MUTUAL: with each other AFFECTION: love

Exercise 3 The Ruined Books

   i. LIFTED: separated BUCKLED: twisted

  ii. BURROWING: going underneath ARBITRARILY: without a plan

Exercise 4 Forest Destruction

   i. SEEMINGLY: appears to be INDESTRUCTIBLE: unbreakable

  ii. PERMANENTLY: for ever STRIPPED: deprived BARE: of everything

 iii. ASTONISHING: amazing VARIETY: different types of

Exercise 5 How Animals became Pets

   i. ACCEPT: tolerate confinement: restriction CONTROL: not having freedom

  ii. INFLUENCE: affect MOVEMENTS: where they could go BEHAVIOUR: what they did

 iii. PREDATOR: hunter PET: domestic animal

Exercise 6 Sharing the Earth

   i. RAPID: quick DISAPPEARANCE: removal SPECIES: types

  ii. RUTHLESS: cruel EXPLOITATION: taking advantage of

 iii. CONFLICTING: opposing ATTITUDES: outlooks

Exercise 7 Threats to Coral Reefs 2

   i. PERIL: danger FULLY: completely REALISED: known

  ii. ENDLESS: (seemed to be) for ever: CONFERENCES: meetings

    TOURS: rounds INSPECTIONS: viewings

 iii. (not) IMPLEMENTED: (not) put into effect

 iv. (governments) ROSE: were appointed (and) FELL: were voted out

  v. FORMED: made (and) DISBANDED: separated

vi. MADE: put forward RECOMMENDATIONS: suggestions

vii. NOT PREPARED: unwilling RESPONSIBILITY: to be the leader
DECISIONS: plans of action

viii. WEALTH: money SACRIFICE: give up CONSERVE: keep

Exercise 8 The Ferry Boat

i. FRENZY: fever IMPATIENCE: did not want to wait

ii. ALARMING: frightening INSTABLLITY: imbalance VESSEL: ship

iii. SCRAMBLED: fought their way THANKFULLY: gratefully

iv. IGNORED: paid no attention to SURROUNDING: going on in the area
PANIC: terror

v. (sat) UPRIGHT: erect GAZED: stared (straight) AHEAD : in front

vi. REMOTE: far away (from the world they) CONTROLLED: ruled

vii. OVERTURNED: capsized MIDSTREAM: in the centre of the river
UNNOTICED: unseen

viii. MODELS: examples DETACHMENT: not involved MODERATION:
not going to extremes

Chapter 19 Combining Information

Exercise 4 Pompeii

i. (a) well watered plain (b) fertile soil (c) gentle climate

Exercise 5 The Rhinoceros

i. (a) they ran away (without being told) (b) they ran in all directions (c) they
dropped equipment

Exercise 6 The Storm

i. (a) they smashed free blocks of marble and (b) flung them aside like pebbles

Exercise 7 After the Storm

i. natural – the melting of ice at the north Pole man-made – extraction of water
from the ground beneath Venice (for use in industrial development

Exercise 8   Protection of the Environment

   i. (a) they will not succeed (b) wealth of expertise (in living memory) will be lost

Exercise 9   Coral Animals

   i. (a) they are responsible for creating the largest structures made by life on earth
      (b) (and yet) they are small

Exercise 10   Emma

   i. (a) her mother phoned (b) an accident on the motorway

  ii. (a) her mother picked an inconvenient time to phone (b) she never forgot her
      her father's birthday

Chapter 20 More exercises in combining questions
Exercise 1   The Great Wall of China

   i. (a) attacked them (b) built barriers

  ii. (a) soldiers (b) local peasants (c) convicted criminals

Exercise 2   Building the Great Wall

   i. (a) long walks on narrow mountain trails (b) colliding with one another

  ii. (a) they carried bricks or stones up the mountain (b) in baskets on their backs

Exercise 3   The Lone Walker

   i. (a) the cold air (b) being alone (c) the square was deserted

  ii. (a) it had been snowing (b) it had rained

Exercise 4   A Thistle Year

   i. (a) the thistles hemmed in their houses (b) and shut out the view all around

  ii. (a) there were thistles all around him (b) his feet were bare

 iii. (a) the thistles were (dead and) dry (b) the days were at their hottest (in December)

Exercise 5   The Destroyed Novel

   i. (a) she had been working for some time (b) she couldn't see Octavia
      (c) Octavia was destructive

  ii. (a) she must have left the door open (b) Lydia's room was always full of nasty objects

 iii. (a) she tore out the pages (b) and threw them around (c) and chewed them

Exercise 6 Benjamin

i. (a) he was a keen reader (b) his favourite subject at school was literature
    (c) he had read this novel over and over again

ii. (a) he finished reading it within a week (b) he read it several times

iii. (a) there was a limited number of spaces (in the class) (b) one of the teachers retired

iv. (a) he acted out key scenes (b) he pretended to be the central character

v. he was writing his own novel [1] so that he could be famous one day [1]

Chapter 21 Appreciating the way writers make use of language

Exercise 4 The Flood

i. to give the idea of devastation / destruction

ii. the movement of the flames

iii. candles are pretty/ gentle/ attractive [1]
     but the situation is serious / ugly / sad / bad [1]

Exercise 5 The Kitchen Table

i. it was like an injury / deep / destructive

ii. the shape (veins) / long and thin [1]
    continues the 'scar' idea // table like a person / personification [1]

iii. different colours / patterns

Exercise 6 The Market in Mumbai

i. he wandered / had no fixed aim /was relaxed [any two for 1 mark each]

ii. he was relaxed / felt he had plenty of time

Exercise 7 Spring

i. change from the unpleasant winter [1]
    to pleasant spring [1] (is like going from unpleasant, difficult terrain to
    pleasant, fertile land)

ii. fertility / plenty of growth / new life

iii. a covering (as a carpet covers a floor)

Exercise 8   The New School

  i. long queues (of girls) [1]

      not a straight line / curved line [1]

 ii. it was strange to them [1]

      they were going to find out about it [1]

iii. to show how many there seemed to be / to show how crowded it was / how overwhelmed she felt

Chapter 22   More exercises in appreciating writers' craft

Exercise 1   The Gardener

  i. he was straining/ it took a lot of effort // he didn't want to do it

 ii. he doesn't want to do the work/ he grudges the effort [1]

      in the same way as a miser doesn't want to part with his money [1]

iii. 'he is like a machine' [1] he seems programmed to do the work / he does it automatically / he is not like a human being [Any 2 of 3 for 1 mark each]

Exercise 2   The Well-Dressed Lady

  i. she looks as if she hasn't thought about how she looks // looks as though she is dressed casually / looks relaxed [1]

      but she has worked hard to create the look / it didn't come naturally/ easily [1]

 ii. the sound is short / artificial // she doesn't really find it funny // she is cynical // it isn't really humour   (Any two for 1 mark each)

Exercise 3   The Mountain Journey

  i. he hasn't been able / free to think properly [1]

      he had to keep his thoughts under control (like an animal under control) [1]

 ii. he was happy / happier

Exercise 4   The Traveller

  i. as if the jungle was wrapped around the path // connotations of death

 ii. it had been easy // he had not been climbing

Exercise 5 Cell Phones

 i. (they seem to) keep people alive / save them (from burdens/ troubles)

 ii. we can be restored / refreshed / relax / take time out [1]

   by getting into a different/ better place / situation (with our cell phone) [1]

 iii. desert

 iv. (cell phones) hurt / destroy (society)

 v. cell phones [1]

   are precious / valuable [1]

Exercise 6 Nizam and Hemu

 i. they shaped them (through their teaching) [1]

   students did not resist / were anxious to learn // it was not hard to influence them [1]

 ii. moulded

 iii. love/ skill/ knowledge (of English / literature)

 iv. they rushed/ were eager/ anxious to get to class

Chapter 23 Quotation questions and vocabulary questions
Exercise 1 The Rain Forests

 i. keenly aware

 ii. foolish

Exercise 2 Climate Change

 i. accelerates

 ii. blazing torches

Exercise 3 Amy

 i. uneasiness

 ii. grimy

Exercise 4 After the Show

 i. stuttering

 ii. (i) stumbling (ii) blundering

Exercise 6 Benjamin

i. sometimes

ii. refused

Exercise 7 Sophie

i. full

ii. afraid

iii. exciting

Exercise 8 Keeping Pavlo Warm

i. copy

ii. opening

iii. other

Exercise 9 World Food Shortage

i. surprising

ii. lack

iii. result

iv. increase

Chapter 24 Combining information in the summary question

Exercise 4 Cafe India

She liked Cafe India because:

i. the coffee was perfect

ii. the service was excellent

iii. the familiarity was comforting

iv. She could sit on the balcony and watch people in the street

v. she could meet friends

vi. she could read novels

vii. she could listen in to other people's conversations

Exercise 5 Children in the Developing World

Ways in which children create wealth in developing countries:

  i.   they work on the land (fields, crops, cattle)

 ii.   they fish

iii.   they do unskilled work (like making carpets)

 iv.   (younger children) collect sticks for firewood

  v.   or drinking water from the well

 vi.   (some boys) might be sent to school and can send back money from their better jobs

vii.   Children help in crises (like drought, famine etc.)

Exercise 6 Children in the Developed World

ways in which children are a financial burden to their parents in a developed country:

  i.   they need a larger house

 ii.   they have increased bill (for food, fuel and clothing)

iii.   children re at school and cannot contribute to the family's finances

 iv.   children expect toys to be bought for them

  v.   and money given for school trips

 vi.   childcare is expensive (when parents are out working)

Exercise 7 A Frightening Experience

The reasons why Salman was terrified:

  i.   the street lights had gone out / it was dark

 ii.   the wind was howling

iii.   he was alone / the streets were deserted

 iv.   it might be later than he thought/ his watch might have stopped and he would get a row at home

  v.   he heard a snuffling sound

 vi.   which got louder and louder

vii.   and something wet brushed against his hand

Exercise 8   Anna

The reasons why Anna was troubled:

i. her relationship with Chris /her boyfriend had come to an end

ii. Chris was going to Australia to study / she wouldn't see him for three years

iii. his parents did not approve of Anna

iv. her parents complained about him

v. and she avoided seeing her parents

vi. her father had to have an operation

vii. she had failed her driving test

Chapter 25   More exercises in summary content points

Exercise 2   Octavia

how the baby became ill, her symptoms, how her mother dealt with the problem:

i. autumn was cold

ii. rain / fog /damp / frost at night (any 1)

iii. she didn't know how to keep the baby warm

iv. baby chewed her gloves, which gave her wet hands

v. and dribbled, which gave her a damp chest

vi. baby caught a cold

vii. coughing at night woke her up

viii. baby wheezed when she breathed

ix. baby's nose was running

xi. baby was spluttering

xi. mother decided / her friend advised her to phone the doctor

xii. and ask for the doctor to visit (rather than take the baby to the doctor)

Exercise 3   The Lonely Lighthouse

The problems which alerted the crew to the fact that something was wrong:

i. there was no welcoming flag

ii. there was no reply to the ship's whistle

iii. there was no movement in or around the lighthouse

iv. there was no response to the rocket

v. there was no response when the sailor called out their names

vi. the gate to the yard was closed

vii. and the door (of the lighthouse) was open

viii. there was no reply to the sailor's (further) shouts

ix. a chair was topples over (in the kitchen)

x. the ashes in the fireplace were cold / there had been no fire was a while

xi. the clock had stopped

xii. the beds were unmade / they had got up (and left) in a hurry

xiii. there was dust on the lamp

xiv. the record was incomplete / not done for several days

xv. there was still no trace of the keepers

Exercise 4 School Uniform

The advantages and disadvantages of school uniform:

i. uniform encourages a sense of belonging / makes students seem like a family

ii. no student is better than another

iii. all students look the same, which levels social groups

iv. students concentrate on studies without worrying about fashion

v. fashion items are kept in good condition

vi. there are no worries about who is the most fashionable

vii. students can be identified outside school

viii. and won't misbehave / will behave well

ix. otherwise they might be in trouble with the school

x. and / or with their parents

xi. good behaviour advertises the school to parents

xii. and makes pupils want to go there / provides role models

xii. but uniform suppresses individuality

xiv. and gives more expense to families

xv. especially poor families

Exercise 5 Titanic

How the actions of various people were responsible for the sinking of Titanic:

    i. not all reports of icebergs reached the control room

    ii. the captain knew it was risky to maintain speed

    iii. but decided to do it anyway

    iv. he didn't want to appear to be timid

    v. or damage his reputation

    vi. the lookouts ignored the possibility of icebergs

    vii. no extra lookouts were posted

    viii. no special instructions were issued to engineers for emergency manoeuvres

    ix. the captain did not consider the possibility of lowing down

    x. because he wanted high speeds for the following day

    xi. the radio operator ignored the warnings (about icebergs) from Californian

    xii. because he did not have experience / judgement

    xiii. the glamour of his job had made him arrogant

Chapter 26 Plan, organise, paragraph and punctuate in summary writing

Exercise 1 Rickshaw Cyclists in Dhaka

    i. they weave in and out of traffic

    ii. they cycle against the oncoming traffic

    iii. the bicycle tyres get dented

    iv. the wheels get scraped

    v. cyclists don't wear helmets

    vi. passengers are not strapped in/ have no safety belts

Exercise 2 Tourists in Sri Lanka

    i. the wonderful climate

    ii. the beauty of the island

iii. the high standard of the hotels

iv. the variety of shops

v. the variety of prices/ everyone can shop there

vi. the good food/ the variety of food

Exercise 4   Punctuation

The moment had arrived. All those weeks of preparation had been moving them towards this day. O level English was a difficult syllabus but the class had had a good teacher. How happy they were about that! All the students filed into the examination hall with butterflies in their stomachs. Was there anyone who was not really nervous? What would the comprehension passage be about this year? Would it be narrative or discursive? Would it suit everyone? Everyone was silent. The papers were give out. They were thinking about what they had been taught about literal comprehension and inferential comprehension, not to forget, of course, the summary question, which carried half of the marks. Everyone started to read the passage but they could not believe their eyes. It was impossible to understand. There was no punctuation whatsoever!

Chapter 27   Writing summaries in Standard English in your own words

Exercise 1   Conjunctions

i. Lucky was very tired because she had been studying sentence structure all day.

ii. When Lucky got home, her mother was there to greet her.

iii. Lucky ate her lunch and went straight to her room to study.

iv. After Lucky revised that day's lesson on sentence structure, she felt very cheerful because she felt she understood how to use conjunctions.

Exercise 2   Relative Pronouns

i. Tulen was an English teacher who worked in a high school in Bangladesh.

ii. Tulen taught English in a high school which had almost five hundred students.

iii. Tulen met one of his former students whom he had taught for three years of high school.

iv. Tulen lived next door to Nath, whose son he had taught for two years of high school.

Exercise 3 Present Participles

Combine the following sentences by using present participles

i. Walking to school, Indrani met an old friend from high school.

ii. Chatting together, they walked along the street.

iii. Hearing that her friend was a teacher, she told her friend that she was a teacher too.

iv. Smiling, her friend told Indrani that she had heard from many colleagues that Indrani was a wonderful teacher.

Chapter 28 More Standard English

Exercise 1 Pavlo 1

It was important for Pavlo to be warm and so we turned up the heating to its highest. We massaged Pavlo's body with warm olive oil. He lay on a cushion, wrapped in cotton wool for warmth. We carried him to the garden every time the sun shone. We gave him a bottle filled with hot water in his bed at night. We give him a drawer in a cabinet in my room which included a piece of fur on which he would curl up. In the early morning, Pavlo kept running into every room to find a better way to keep himself warm. He liked to crawl inside the shade and sit next to the bulb which was in the sitting room. He enjoyed drinking warm milk. In winter we had to be careful to ensure that the windows were closed to preventing Pavlo being caught in the cold. In the first warm days in spring, Pavlo went into the garden.

Exercise 2 Pavlo 2

It was important for Pavlo to be warm so that he would not feel the difference from the climate of South America. It also played a part in the health of the marmoset. As the prophecies made about the animal were going to be realised within six months, the family started to take them seriously by surrounding him in cotton wool for warmth. Olive oil was also used by the family to keep the tiny body of Pavlo warm by massaging him. They also put his cushion in every patch of sunlight. To help him sleep at night, they gave him a bottle filled with hot water during the cold winter and also in summer. The family had to push the drawer closed for extra warmth. The writer's sister even bought a baby blanket for Pavlo to keep him warm and he liked to jump into the bed, searching for heat. Of the types of heating they had, Pavlo preferred the electric lamp.

Exercise 3   The Lighthouse 1

The ship's crew noticed immediately that something was wrong because there was no welcoming flag flying from the lighthouse when the ship was near. A whistle and a rocket were used, but still there was no response from those lighthouse keepers. The gates that should have been open were closed and the door of the lighthouse was wide open. The fire had not been lit for some time. The last entry of the lighthouse record book was the fifteenth of December. This puzzled the searchers. The lamp was covered with dust, showing that it also had not been lit for some time, and the beds were unmade. Two of the three sets of waterproof clothing were missing from the cupboard. The grass along the edge of the cliff was torn away when they investigated outside the lighthouse. The railings around the platform where the crane stood were broken. A huge boulder which was part of the cliff had been moved a great distance down the staircase and was blocking it.

Exercise 4   The Lighthouse 2

The ship's crew noticed immediately that something was wrong because the welcoming flag should have been waving for their welcome. They thought that the keepers might be busy working out of sight. The whistle was blown to call the keepers but there was no response. The ship's captain ordered his crew to fire a rocket but it didn't make the keepers notice them. A small group of sailors was ordered to check the area. They found out that the warning lamp was in working order and, when they checked the record book, it hadn't been filled in for eleven days. The sailors told their captain that they hadn't found the keepers. The next day they searched the lighthouse and found out that two of the three sets of waterproof clothing were missing. The railing around the platform was broken and a huge boulder was moved down the stairway. There was no trace of the three keepers. All the crew of the ship thought there was a mystery.

Exercise 5   The Lighthouse 3

The ship's crew noticed immediately that something was wrong because there was no welcoming flag flying from the shore. The captain asked them to send a rocket over the island but still nothing was seen of the keepers. Some sailors were ordered to find out what had happened ashore. They started calling the keepers' names and there was no answer. The entrance gate was closed, but it should have been opened by the keepers for their arrival. The main door was open and again they called the names of the keepers. In the kitchen too, chairs stood next to the table and one of them was knocked over and lying on its side. The beds were unmade and it seemed that the occupants had just risen from them and left hurriedly. There was dust over the warning lamp. They found that two sets of waterproof clothing were missing and one still hung there. They also found that the grass had been torn away along the top edge of the cliff.

Exercise 6   Threats to Coral Reefs 1

When hotel developers near coral reefs compete for land, they raise its price and as a result force local people to leave their homes. In fact, in some places, hotels have been built on burial sites on the coast. Little by little the construction of golf courses for tourists has proved fatal to coral reefs as the golf courses are treated by large amounts of water and also by fertilisers and pesticides, which contain deadly loads of waste materials and chemicals. Airport runways are built and their construction produces too much waste, which is sufficient to kill coral. The destruction of coral means that local people are short of food. The increase of pollution, noise and roads, and also the destruction of the natural habitats of animals, have been caused by the arrival of tourists. Sailing ships create severe damage on coral reefs with their heavy anchors. Coral continues to be damaged by submarines and divers also damage coral reefs considerably.

Exercise 7   Threats to Coral Reefs 2

When hotel developers near coral reefs compete for land they force local people out of their homes. It is easy to understand the location of hotels in these magnificent areas but the way of life of the country is exploited to a great extent. Tourist attractions like golf courses deprive the local people of shorelines which are necessary for their way of life. Pollution is an important factor in the destruction of wonderful coastal areas. Pollutants are dumped on the coral reefs, which destroys life in the reefs. The rock from coral reefs has been used on a small scale to build houses but the rocks are now being excavated in large quantities for hotel development, yet again depriving the local people of their own houses. Lagoons are being dug deeper, affecting the area where fish breed, and the prices of popular fish has been raised so high that the people cannot afford them. Boats that carry people cause severe damage to reefs.

Exercise 8   Threats to Coral Reefs 3

When hotel developers compete for land they force local people out of their homes. The country is frequently exploited for tourist entertainment. The construction of golf courses for tourists deprives local people of coastal areas. The water used by golf courses drains out on the coral reefs and carries a deadly load of chemicals. Airports are built along the coast on coral reefs. Their construction produces large quantities of waste. Rock from coral reefs is taken in uncontrolled quantities to build tourist hotels, thus depriving local people of building material. Pleasure boats destroy the areas where fish breed, depriving local people of food. Some fish are too expensive because they can only be afforded by tourists. Villages are destroyed by pollution created by tourists. Huge jetties and docks are built over coral reefs and hotels often lack proper sewage facilities. Boats carry people to dive, which increases the destruction of coral. Everyday boats send their anchors crashing down on reefs.